Sister Wendy

on

Prayer

Sister Wendy

on

Prayer

SISTER WENDY BECKETT

Biographical Introduction by David Willcock

Harmony Books
New York

Copyright © 2006 by Sister Wendy Beckett
Biographical introduction copyright © 2006 by David Willcock

Published in the United States by Harmony Books, an imprint of the Crown
Publishing Group, a division of Random House, Inc., New York.
www.crownpublishing.com

Harmony Books is a registered trademark and the Harmony Books colophon
is a trademark of Random House, Inc.

Originally published in Great Britain by Continuum, London, in 2006.

Library of Congress Cataloging-in-Publication Data

Beckett, Wendy.
    Sister Wendy on prayer / Wendy Beckett ; biographical introduction by
David Willcock.
    p. cm.
    1. Prayer—Christianity.   2. Spiritual life—Christianity.   I. Willcock,
David.   II. Title.
    BV210.3.B43 2007
    248.3'2—dc22   2007015218

ISBN 978-0-307-39381-4

Printed in the United States of America

Design by Sarah Maya Gubkin

10 9 8 7 6 5 4 3 2 1

First American Edition

Contents

SECTION 1: THE PRACTICE OF PRAYER

Contents

Section 2: prayer and belief

For David, without whose help
this book could not have been written

Sister Wendy
on
Prayer

Introduction

I always like writing about art. Quite apart from the beauty of the pictures, which can distract you from any inadequacies on the part of the text, we are really dealing only with opinions. I am telling you that this is what I think. What do you think? If you take another look at any work of art — a long look — and find you disagree with me, I am only too pleased.

Writing about prayer is very different. These are not just my personal opinions, these are my convictions about what is deepest in our lives, most integral to being human: our relationship with God. What I write here, in however faltering a fashion, I feel to be so true that (forgive the melodrama) I would be prepared to die for it.

I am very well aware that what I write about prayer is not to everyone's liking. There seems to be a universal certainty that there is some secret about prayer that can be taught. People feel sure that they would be prepared to go to a great deal of trouble and experience considerable difficulties if that was the way to uncover this mysterious "secret." But prayer is essentially simple.

I cannot but recall the biblical story of Naaman the leper. You will remember that he came from Syria to be healed by the prophet Elisha. Naaman had clear expectations about how the miracle would happen. Elisha would come out to meet him, there would be blessings and ceremonial prayers, incense. He was completely disconcerted and very much annoyed when all his expectations were confounded. Elisha merely sent him a message telling him to bathe seven times in the Jordan. He was all for packing up and returning to Syria (far better rivers there too), when the persuasions of his servants, who obviously liked him, encouraged him to do as the prophet had said. Reluctant and disgruntled, Naaman took off his clothes as he would for any bath, and waded seven times into the river. When he came out, his leprosy had disappeared (2 Kings 5:1–14).

The point of the story is that he very nearly missed his miracle because the instructions were so simple. Evidently we do not like simplicity — no room there for excuse. Furthermore, he had to do it himself. Elisha did not come out and pass on the magic secret. It was all up to Naaman, a responsibility which he was as unwilling to incur as any of us are. It seems to me that we have here a good parallel with our attitude to prayer and our difficulty in accepting the nakedness of its simplicity.

The irony is that when Naaman accepted that no one could help him, that he alone must go down into the water, his bit was done. It was neither Naaman nor Elisha who worked the miracle. It was God. When we accept that no one can help us, that we alone must stand there in prayer, our responsibility ends. It is not we who pray, it is God. Prayer is His business. I was going to say from start to finish, but obviously the starting must be our own choice, our own decision. We have to will to let God take possession and stay in that will whatever happens or, more likely, does not happen. Nothing happened to Naaman in the Jordan. He had to persevere with his seven dips, and only then, as he came out, did his leprosy fall away from him.

If we want it enough, we can live permanently in those sanctifying waters. But at the beginning it will be enough to go in and come out and always be ready to return. As we know from the Gospels, Jesus regards seven as a rather elastic figure ("I do not say to you seven times, but seventy times seven," Matthew 18:21).

I have found this book very difficult to write. This is partly because I myself have been so exceptionally fortunate, being privileged to live in solitude and spend many hours a day in pure prayer. I have been tempted to think that my privilege invalidates anything I say. But surely this cannot be so. Prayer is for all of us. No one is fully human who has not some sort of relationship with God, even an anonymous relationship. A sense of the mystery in which we live (why are we here? who are we? what is the meaning of being me rather than you?) is integral to the human consciousness, and it is to that awareness that I would give the name of prayer. It may be rudimentary, but it may also be the only kind of prayer of which an individual is capable, the only way God can come to that person.

For those who have experienced even the most fleeting moments of this "contact" with God, as well as for those who wish to make or have made a profound lifelong surrender to Him in prayer, I think what I have written here holds good. It may be frightening — in fact, I know it is. But fear must never keep us back from allowing God to draw us into fulfillment.

Biographical Introduction

BY DAVID WILLCOCK

In Saint John's Gospel, Jesus exhorts his disciples to be "in the world, but not of it." Surely nothing acts as a better summary or description of the career of Sister Wendy Beckett.

Sister Wendy has led not one but two extraordinary lives. She entered a convent sixty years ago at the age of sixteen. And for the last thirty-five years, she has lived the austere life of a hermit, gladly undergoing the sort of solitary confinement that has been used to break hardened criminals and political detainees. But then another vocation has been superimposed onto this monastic rigor: that of a television art critic.

In 1991, Sister Wendy, the "art nun," was thrust into the limelight. She offered in her television programs a spiritual resource for a largely secular society. And offscreen, to those she met along the way, she offered refreshingly uncomplicated and sometimes unconventional spirituality that was a source of fascination and inspiration. Resolutely agnostic producers, world-weary crews and hard-bitten press men could all be found, once the cameras were wrapped, pressing for answers to deeply felt questions about life, God, prayer and religion. This intense interest was further echoed by passersby and viewers.

As Sister Wendy has indicated above, she sees prayer as terrifyingly simple and deeply personal. There are no tricks, no tips, no secret shortcuts: prayer is a matter between God and the believer. That conviction, combined with her unique lifestyle, has always led her to maintain stoutly that her views on prayer would be of no interest to, or would have no application for, anyone else. It is only the evident interest and repeated questions of others that have persuaded her to break silence on this most intimate subject.

Even then she has resisted a thesis that presupposes a coherent "answer" to prayer in general. Instead, this book is a summary of her thoughts, a series of her personal answers to some of the frequently asked questions that have arisen from believers, fellow travelers and those with no faith or religion. They are presented as meditations to be read through or dipped into at will. Each meditation is intended not to put an end to questions, but to provoke further thought and always, always, to leave the last word to God.

Wendy Mary Beckett was born in Johannesburg, South Africa, on February 25, 1930, but she spent her early childhood in Scotland. Her father, Aubrey, took his family there so that he could study medicine at Edinburgh University. They lived outside the city in a village called Colinton. It was here, while still too young to pinpoint precise dates, but probably aged three or four, that Wendy had what she now describes as the defining moment of her life. Seventy or more years later, she remembers it with Proustian vividness:

> *It was a Sunday morning: we always had sausages for breakfast on a Sunday, and a glorious aroma of hot sausage filled the house. We were living in a little village outside Edinburgh. The local regiment had their barracks there, and they used to march past our house on church parade on Sunday mornings.*
>
> *For some reason I was sitting under the table. I could smell the sausages, I could hear the band, I could feel the carpet. And I became conscious of God. It was an overwhelming experience of greatness and of goodness and of protection. I remember feeling with wonder that the world — so bewildering to a little child — made sense, that it was God's world and I was a blessed child within it. If you ask how I knew, I cannot tell you. I saw nothing and I heard nothing. But from then on God was always with me, the center of all I did, giving it significance.*

At the time, Wendy never spoke of this epiphany (my word, not hers). She did not mention it to her mother or father because, like most small children, she assumed her experience was normal. It was only later that she realized that many (even most) people go through life without ever experiencing anything like this. She still has no "explanation" for why this grace should have been given to her particularly, and she is still shy of talking about it, as though no words can ever encompass the mystery of what happened to her. Indeed, she says, "I would love to be able to describe it even to myself, because this certainty of utter love and safety is unutterably precious." What is clear is that this one experience has shaped her entire life and thought. In looking at the serene confidence in God in sections such as God's Business (page 35) and Peace (page 120), we can see that this is someone who has seen at a very deep level that "this is one of the consequences of prayer: the safety, the freedom, because essentially we have nothing to fear."

Because of this deep-seated conviction, Sister Wendy's vocation as a nun also dates back to her very earliest years. She says simply that she cannot remember a time when she did *not* want to be a nun. Her decision does not seem to have surprised anyone. When her cousin Daphne dramatically announced her intention to take the veil, it caused a family confrontation that went down in Beckett family legend as The Day When Daph Told Us. But with Wendy it seems to have been tacitly assumed, at least by her mother, Dorothy, that this was what she was destined for once school was ended. On her father's return from serving as a medical officer with the RAF in the Second World War, he voiced concern that Wendy should first get a degree, but was firmly told (in an overheard conversation), "She's a difficult child, Aubrey, and she's set her heart on this."

Both Dr. and Mrs. Beckett were devout Catholics. Having moved back to South Africa from Edinburgh after Wendy's father had qualified as a doctor, they sent Wendy and her younger sister, Pamela, to a Catholic school. It was run by the order of Notre Dame de Namur. And therein lay a hidden flaw in the young Miss Beckett's idealistic dream of living a quiet life of prayer and devotion to God.

Religious orders exist on different scales of engagement with the world. Some orders of nuns, such as the Carmelites, are contemplative. They live a life of prayer and contemplation enclosed within their convent. Other orders are active, praying and saying the offices but also working in the world as teachers, nurses or missionaries. Notre Dame is one such order. Girls who feel a vocation would normally seek out an order suited to their personalities. The young Wendy Beckett was so dreamily sure of her generic vocation to be a nun that this process of finding the right order seems not to have occurred to her at all. If it had, an active order would surely not have been her choice. By her own account, Wendy was impractical, studious, sedentary — an avid reader but not a doer. One of her earliest photographs is of the two-year-old Wendy sitting in a wheelbarrow. Her mother has captioned it: "There is nothing Wendy likes better than being pushed around in a wheelbarrow."

Today no religious order would consider taking a teenage aspirant. Anyone thinking about a vocation is thoroughly vetted to see if he or she is suitable before being allowed to commit to lifetime vows of poverty, chastity and obedience. In 1947 recruitment was far less rigorous. And so it was that one month before her seventeenth birthday, Wendy Beckett left her home in South Africa for good, unaware that this momentous step would commit her, like her teachers, not to a life of silence in the cloister, but to the rough-and-tumble of the classroom.

English-speaking Notre Dame novices were all trained in the UK, at the novitiate in Ashdown, East Sussex. Commercial air travel was only just beginning after the Second World War. Rather than leave their unchaperoned daughter exposed on a long sea voyage, the Becketts paid for first-class airfare. Ironically, a violent storm nearly downed the plane and led to an extended stopover in Cairo in addition to the numerous refueling stops along the way. With a purse crammed with high-denomination banknotes, the earnest young woman traveled in style, innocently delighting porters along the route with tips equivalent to a month's wages. When the sister who had come to accompany her to the convent bought economy rail tickets, Wendy patiently explained, "I'm sure Daddy wouldn't want me to travel second class."

Travel at the rear of the train was the least of the shocks that her new life would be inflicting on Sister Wendy, or rather, Sister Michael of Saint Peter. Like members of the British actors' union Equity, all members of a religious order in 1947 had to have a unique name so they could be identified. A candidate could choose her name or even keep her own, provided it was a saint's name and did not already belong to another member of the order. The first criterion ruled out Wendy, a name that had been invented by J. M. Barrie for his *Peter Pan* heroine. Wendy was actually glad to be rid of what she thought was a flaccid and silly name, but which new name would she choose? Within the order the elegant names of female saints were the most popular, with lots of Marys and Bernadettes qualified by another name. So the now nameless young South African chose two strong warrior saints: Saint Michael, the angel who defeats the devil, and to differentiate her from any other Sister Michaels already in the order — a second pugnacious saint's name, Saint Peter.

The novitiate years were no problem for an essentially quiet and obedient young woman. The order of life for trainee active nuns was very similar to a contemplative order. Novices were kept away from the world, but even at this stage Sister Wendy was the odd one out. For many other novices the vow of celibacy was a real and painful emotional sacrifice, and like mini-Marias from *The Sound of Music*, obedience came only after repeated reprimands for high-spirited breaking of the rules of silence and order. In contrast, Wendy was completely unaffected by giving up a world of boys, marriage and childbirth, and so compliant that the novice mistress was suspicious of her preternatural obedience to the rules. Where other nuns were gregarious at recreation, Wendy's lasting friends came from before her entry to the convent: her cousin Daphne (she of The

Day . . .), Coz, who entered Notre Dame somewhat later, and her school friend Val, with whom Sister Wendy corresponded until Val's recent death.

Enrolling in a teaching order of nuns at least ensured that Wendy Beckett got a first-rate education. Notre Dame needed their most able nuns to be qualified. Midway through the twentieth century, it was still not taken for granted that young women would have equality of education, but in 1950, Sister Michael of Saint Peter was sent by the order to Oxford to read English at St. Anne's College.

University for a nun was strictly limited to academic attainment. For lay students, going to Oxford means not only books and lectures, but a packed life of new friendships, plays, societies, rowing, parties and punting amid beautiful architecture, sculpted gardens and willow-fringed rivers. Such temptations were out of bounds for Sister Michael of Saint Peter. The young sister was closely guarded to preserve her modesty and prevent any temptation to stray from her vocation. Where most young women stayed in halls of residence, she was sent to live in the Notre Dame convent on Woodstock Road in Oxford. This Victorian redbrick building is about half a mile up the road from St. Anne's College. Her college life consisted solely of attending the offices and mass at the convent, walking down the road to tutorials at St. Anne's — a pleasant walk but far from the "dreaming spires" of the city center — and attending lectures. She was not allowed to join any university society or to wander round the city for recreation. She spoke only to her tutor in weekly tutorials and managed to pass all three years of her degree without having a single conversation with a fellow student. For many this would seem to be a severe deprivation, but Sister Wendy still speaks with affection of her romantic Oxford experience. Not speaking to a "real" student ensured that the glamorous mental edifice she built of Oxford remained unsullied by less than perfect human experience.

Instead, Sister Michael lived in an idealistic dream and inhabited a world of books. Free of all external distractions, she delighted her tutors with the breadth and depth of her reading. She must be one of the first students ever to have completed a vacation reading list. She is still a voracious and omnivorous reader, consuming serious literature, religious books, academic works on art and, for relaxation, quantities of lurid murder mysteries, which she loves for their sense of justice: evil always gets its comeuppance. In the passage on The Scriptures (page 74) in this book, she takes it for granted that anyone who is serious about their faith and about prayer will want to inform both through intelligent reading. But not everyone will be able to read as much she does. Both television researchers and this particular producer found her ability to read a three-hundred-page book on a short-hop plane trip impressive and sometimes intimidating. But at university it served her well. Sister Michael received Oxford's highest accolade, a

Congratulatory First. Professor J. R. R. Tolkien led the applause at her viva voce.

The two-year novitiate in deepest Sussex, where the novices led a de facto contemplative life with no outside contact, and the silent degree at Oxford were an extended honeymoon period. It was only afterward, when Sister Michael of Saint Peter was returned to South Africa to teach in Notre Dame schools, that the implications of her rash choice of order sank in. She found herself a square peg in a very round hole. After taking a teaching diploma in Liverpool in 1954, the Oxford graduate with the starred first found herself teaching in schools without advanced curriculum, living in convents where the only books were Enid Blyton and children's stories, and, worst of all, where the monastic discipline allowed for only two half-hour periods of private prayer a day.

For anyone who wants to pray there is the inevitable clash between the active life of work, family and friends, and the passive space needed to pray. But for most of us the failure to create quiet time is more often about a lack of willpower, our own refusal to reorder our personal list of priorities. In Sister Wendy's case there was no free will possible. Although she felt the need for more time for private, silent prayer, it was simply not allowed. For good reasons, religious orders have their own rules of life and timetables. They do not permit the setting of personal agendas. In retrospect, Sister Wendy claims that the discipline of obedience to the demands of the order over the years was invaluable, a sloughing off of the hard skin of selfishness. But it is clear that at times the process was truly painful.

> When I asked if I could have a little extra time for private prayer, I was told, "If you've got spare time, you can go out into the playground and pick up the children's wastepaper. You've got all the prayer you need: half an hour in the morning and half an hour in the evening. A good sister of Notre Dame doesn't need more prayer." This was one of the very few times in my life when I have cried. Not because she'd said no, but because she thought I was a religious maniac. I remember saying to God, "Well, at least I'm your religious maniac. I don't want to be unbalanced, but if I am, just help me to be a loving maniac."

It may take just two paragraphs to summarize, but this process of realization and negotiation lasted for twenty years. Though exchanges like this clearly left their mark, the Notre Dame sister did her best to support the order she had chosen. After all, it was not Notre Dame's fault that their rule and ethos did not fit with the spiritual discipline that Sister Wendy felt she needed. And though this spiritual thirst left her incomplete, she was by no means an outsider for those twenty years.

Besides teaching in local schools in South Africa, Sister Michael of Saint Peter also lectured at Witwatersrand University. She became a reverend mother within the order. And she also became Wendy again. When the Second

Vatican Council liberalized religious orders, Sister Wendy
took up her own name. She describes this as a "penance."
She actually preferred being known as two male saints, but
believing herself to be "a real Wendy: essentially silly," she
thought it would be better for her not to hide her true
nature behind a saintly masculine carapace, much to the
future relief of television producers who might otherwise
have had to promote a series called *Sister Michael of Saint
Peter's Story of Painting*. But all this time, under whichever
name, she was asking periodically and repeatedly to be
allowed to transfer to a contemplative order. When she
speaks in Silence (page 45) of gathering up "flinders of
time" for prayer, there is the pain of experience behind the
exhortation.

In 1970, Sister Wendy experienced a series of epileptic
seizures. A doctor diagnosed stress as the root cause of
these. Notre Dame realized that radical action needed to
be taken. A letter arrived giving permission for Sister
Wendy to live a contemplative life. Rather than living a
"freelance" life as a contemplative Notre Dame nun completely against the spirit of the order, it was decided that
she should leave and become a hermit. She had been in
touch with the Carmelite Order, and a Carmelite convent
in Norfolk offered to let her live within its grounds. With
the permission of the bishop she became officially a Consecrated Virgin under the protection of the Sisters of the
Carmelite Order.

Consecrated Virgins are an ancient order in the church, built on the example of holy women in the early Christian centuries, many of whom were martyrs like Saint Agatha, whose picture by Tiepolo Sister Wendy contemplates in Suffering II (page 65). Catholic canon law adds the Consecrated Virgins to other forms of consecrated religious life "through their pledge to follow Christ more closely, virgins are consecrated to God, mystically espoused to Christ and dedicated to the service of the Church, when the diocesan Bishop consecrates them according to the approved liturgical rite" (Canon 604).

Many Consecrated Virgins live an active celibate life in the world and wear everyday clothes. Because of her unique vocation to be a hermit, Sister Wendy chose to keep the monastic simplicity that she was used to. Her identity was completely bound up in being a nun, so when the Carmelite monastery at Quidenham invited her to live in their grounds, she put herself voluntarily under obedience to the Carmelite mother superior. So that she would not have to worry about what clothes to wear, she designed her own unique monastic garb, which has elements taken from three separate religious orders. She wears a veil, again to simplify life; there are no worries about hairstyles if one shaves one's head. And she lives her own rule of life.

Before the bishop would give his permission, Sister Wendy had to be checked out just in case she really was a "loving maniac" filled with good intentions but psychically unable to take the strain of living on her own. She was interviewed by a Jesuit priest who asked how she saw her life as a hermit. From the depths of one of the voluminous pockets that religious habits conceal, she produced a crumpled piece of paper with her proposed daily schedule. This document specified and limited her hours of prayer and included work and a daily walk for exercise. The Jesuit immediately pronounced that she was the "real thing" and told her never to depart from her plan. With minor modifications that she mentions in Commonsense Prayer (page 41), the life sketched out on that piece of paper is the schedule she follows today.

The tiny village of Quidenham is hidden deep in the countryside of Norfolk, England, about thirty minutes from Norwich. It boasts an ancient round-towered parish church and a mound that local legend claims as Queen Boudicca's burial place, but it is far from any tourist trail. The Carmelite sisters occupy Quidenham Hall, a manor house first mentioned in the Domesday Book as belonging to one Guy, or Guido, who gave his name to Guidenham. Passed down through various aristocratic families, the earls of Albermarle donated the rambling mansion, built on that medieval core, to the Carmelite order in 1948.

The community lives in Carmel. Carmel is marked by a wall that extends around the convent, even symbolically intersecting the parlors — in the form of a wooden rail — where sisters meet visitors and relatives. Beyond the walled house is the estate: a stream crossed by a beautiful hump-back bridge and acres of fields grazed by sheep. Well away from the house, in the middle of a dense evergreen spin-ney, is the caravan, or trailer, that serves as Sister Wendy's hermitage.

Trailer is a misnomer. This is no Hollywood-style Win-nebago. It is, in fact, a Portakabin, the sort of thing used by site managers on building sites as a shelter from the ele-ments. This is Sister Wendy's second hermitage. When she arrived in 1971, she lived in a really battered green camper, the sort in which British families spend cramped and belea-guered summer holidays. But when a leak in the roof became unstoppable, the sisters insisted that this modern version should take its place.

But even the trailer Mark 2 model is far from the lap of luxury. Like Sister Wendy's habit and hair, her living condi-tions are sparsely functional, designed to streamline her life. Beyond the thin metal door there is the bare minimum of furniture: a desk, a table, a chair, a bed and a window with a view of trees and a glimpse of fields. There is no radio, television, telephone, fax or computer. The only clue to Sister Wendy's career is in the countless postcards and reproductions of art propped up on every conceivable surface, each one providing an invitation to meditation as she lives out her day.

That day begins while most of the population, including the neighboring sisters, are asleep. She gets up at 1:30 a.m.

It used to be 3:30, but her body clock has now pushed the time two hours earlier. This is a source of great fascination for people who meet her: people with jobs, families, televisions and plans for the evening. It is like meeting someone who has stepped off a long-haul flight and forgotten to adjust her body clock to the new time zone. But as Sister Wendy makes clear in Commonsense Prayer, this is not spiritual heroism. Her early rising is matched by an equally early bedtime. This is not sleep deprivation, but a pragmatic way of ensuring that she is not disturbed. The silent hours of the night are broken by no sounds apart from the occasional owl hoot. This is when Sister Wendy, sustained by two or three cups of strong white coffee, fits in the majority of her seven hours of contemplative prayer.

At 6:30 a.m. she makes her way up to the monastery. In a deserted anteroom the sisters leave out her food for the day: cold vegetables, skimmed milk and one slice of rye bread. They also leave out yesterday's newspaper, so that the hermit can keep track of what is going on in the world. After scanning the news and devouring sports and the obituaries, Sister Wendy loads her rations into her basket, collects her share of post from the monastery foyer and sets off for the highlight of her day: mass.

As she makes clear in The Sacrament (page 70), the unequivocal, objective grace promised by God in the Eucharist is a lifeline for Sister Wendy. It is her spiritual fuel. It is literally the center of her life, God's unconditional grace given daily to sustain her arduous vocation. When she started working with the BBC, the only extra demand in her contract was that the production team should work the filming schedule around daily mass wherever they were in the world.

But even in the celebration of the Lord's Supper, Sister Wendy's hermit status is symbolically maintained. For the duration of the service Sister Wendy sits apart and unseen in an alcove of the monastery church known as the belfry. She sees the priest and the Carmelite sisters only as they share the bread and the wine.

By 8:30 a.m., then, the most important part of Sister Wendy's day is over. With her basket of food and post she returns to her trailer in the woods. She sees no one, and talks to no one unless there is a need for urgent communication. There is one sister, nominated by the community, who will deliver telephone messages if they are necessary for work or health and who occasionally helps Sister Wendy with awkward manual tasks, such as shaving her head with a razor (hair growing under a wimple is itchy and uncomfortable).

This silent day is broken only by the meager lunch of cold vegetables, skimmed milk and rye bread. On major feast days such as Easter there might be hot vegetables and a fish finger, heated in an antiquated Baby Belling oven. The occasional gift of a bottle of wine is eked out a glass a day until it goes sour. Otherwise, until the day ends with a bath and medicines (for heart problems and to guard against her epilepsy) at 6:30 p.m., the time is filled with more periods of contemplation and work.

Even contemplative nuns and hermits must earn a living. Saint Benedict wrote work into his first monastic rule as a guard against religious excesses. The Carmelite sisters write books, produce postcards and notecards with their own art and photography and run a guesthouse for retreats. Sister Wendy kept the same philosophy with her own schedule, which built in work to provide a necessary balance in a life of solitude.

The work she took on, however, could hardly be considered light relief. Few outside the world of twelfth-century scholarship can know much about John, who became abbot of the Cistercian monastery of Ford in southwest England in 1194. Fewer still can have dipped into the medieval Latin of his *Sermons on the Final Verses of the Song of Songs.* Thanks to the English translation completed by Sister Wendy Mary Beckett in 1977, anyone interested can go to Amazon.com and buy it — all seven volumes.

Medieval Latin translation is hard, meticulous work, and it was a contributing factor to another bout of illness in the 1980s that rendered Sister Wendy unable to continue. While recuperating, she asked the mother superior of the Carmelite sisters (under whom she has placed herself in voluntary obedience) if instead of her regular translation work, she could study art. It was a turning point.

After a while, thinking she should be earning her keep,

Sister Wendy wrote a book, *Contemporary Women Artists*. She started contributing to the magazine *Modern Painters*. Postcards and art books started mounting up in the trailer — so much so that further into Sister Wendy's art criticism career, there was a near disaster when a book mountain collapsed onto her when she was asleep. In response, the community insisted on building a brick library next to the trailer. Windowless and resembling an outdoor privy, it nonetheless provides a more permanent and weatherproof home for Sister Wendy's books than she herself enjoys.

Readers relished Sister Wendy's unconventional and refreshingly personal approach to art. Those readers included scouts from the television industry on the lookout for talent that might transfer from page to screen. A researcher from the BBC, Randall Wright, persuaded Sister Wendy to take part in a documentary about the National Gallery. When the program was transmitted, the controller of BBC2 rang the film's director and memorably told him to "give that nun a series."

It might seem strange that a woman who had begged for so long to live as a contemplative should choose to thrust herself into the active and largely unreflective world of the media. Like joining the Notre Dame order, her decision was due more to enthusiasm than informed choice. Later her motives for continuing to present television programs, supported by the sisters (who watched her programs at special screenings on video and television brought to the monastery by the producers), were to open people's eyes to a spiritual aspect of life in a secular world through the beauty of art.

> *There was no big "should I give up the caravan to do television? Am I spoiling my hermit life?" I really didn't think it was anything. I thought it was just a weekend here or there. What did it matter really if it was going to be useful? Of course, it turned out to be very much more, but I didn't know that. So I was saved. I'm naturally so selfish I might well have said no.*

Working in television proved far more costly in time and energy than she could ever have anticipated. She persisted with the sacrifice, and throughout her adopted cuckoo second career, Sister Wendy consistently referred to the camper at Quidenham as her "real life." What we might call the real world was a strange, sometimes confusing, sometimes frightening experience. The startling gaps in Sister Wendy's cultural map emphasized that this was a woman who was "in the world, but not of it." For instance, she had never seen *It's a Wonderful Life,* which she was persuaded to watch one Thanksgiving in Chicago. She turned it off halfway through, appalled at James Stewart shouting at his children ("Such a bad example").

Even in the midst of the frenetic world of television production, Sister Wendy's life of prayer continued. When she speaks of Prayer in Everyday Life (page 42), there is experience not only of the hermitage but of carving solitude and quietness out of the chaos of modern technological life. She continued to rise early, though the energy demanded for filming meant that on location Sister Wendy would get up as late as 4:00 or 5:00 a.m., surprising sleepy night porters across Europe and America in a quest for early morning coffee. But she also snatched silent moments from the busiest situations, gathering silence around her like a cloak.

Take a typical filming day in an art gallery closed to the public. It takes about an hour to set the lights to film one painting. The house lights are switched off. The gallery is dark apart from a bright bulb of light and activity around the artwork, where the crew busy themselves with shadows, flares and exposures. Beyond this glowing pool of activity the unmistakable form of Sister Wendy sits hunched on a low-slung bench. Although she is seated in a direct line of sight to the painting or sculpture, she is utterly still. Her eyes are tight shut. It is as though she is creating a personal minihermitage within the echoing vaults of the gallery as she concentrates, motionless, until everything is ready for her to step into the light and deliver her piece to the camera. For some people this stillness and aloneness can be disquieting. In society, sitting so obviously apart for such a concentrated period signifies unhappiness, distress or illness. With the best of intentions, or out of social awkwardness, those unused to Sister Wendy's way of working feel moved to offer help; they try to be friendly and offer to keep her company.

But for Wendy, this utter stillness is entirely normal. Indeed, her favorite part of the whole filming process is the taking of room tone. This is the moment when, at the end of filming a sequence, the sound man asks for quiet and records thirty seconds of the background atmosphere to ease transitions in editing. As everyone else on the crew waits motionless and silent for the all clear, but with barely concealed impatience, Sister Wendy sits transfused with the happiness of someone who has just had a message from home. It is significant that the painting by Gentileschi, which she chooses to talk about in Silence II (page 46), is of an active musician frozen into an image of stillness.

The most important continuity between life in the hermitage and her art programs is the lifeline of daily mass. Even if attendance had not been a contractual obligation, the sacrament was so clearly vital to Sister Wendy that production and crew swiftly realized it was also a priority for getting the best performance from "the talent." If there were less than noble motives at first, there were soon more than enough volunteers to accompany Sister Wendy every morning, people without any specific religion finding this contemplative space in the filming day an unexpected refreshment.

Not that the process of getting to mass was necessarily calm. Every move to a new location required military-style planning to find the nearest Catholic church with a suitable mass timetable. But mistakes happened, and faced with the alternative of missing divine sustenance, Sister

Wendy proved capable of worldly pragmatism. One researcher negotiating the complex medieval streets of Toledo early in the morning found the cathedral elusive, always one block away in a fiendish one-way system. As the time for the kyrie drew ever nearer, Sister Wendy urged her to drive the wrong way up a (deserted) one-way street and park in the plaza right outside. They emerged from mass to find their car swallowed up by a sea of café tables in a pedestrianized tourist zone.

Although Sister Wendy clearly has the capacity for solitude to a degree that most of us would find unbearable, she has none of the marks of a loner. Off duty after filming, she can be convivial, chatty. She laughs easily. She is socially adept and plunges readily into conversation with anyone from museum curators and internationally acclaimed artists to hotel porters, waiters and, lowest of the low, television producers. And she consistently undermines people's preconceptions about what a conventional nun should be like.

Her matter-of-fact attitude toward the body shocked many who automatically expect all religious people to be prudes. The phrase that really shot her to prominence came when discussing a Stanley Spencer painting in Liverpool: "I particularly like two things: the pattern of the wallpaper and her lovely fluffy pubic hair." Sister Wendy admits now that if she had been more media aware at the time, she might not have said it, but she defends her orthodoxy to the hilt. If God created the body, there is no part of it that is dirty, sinful or unclean. It is only human attitudes and human minds that make it so.

Wendy does not see herself as a polemicist or theologian with a vocation to discuss Church doctrine. There is nothing in this book that contradicts the teaching of the Church or that differs from other Catholic thinkers, such as her great hero and role model, the medieval hermit Mother Julian of Norwich. But she does not stand on social or ecclesiastical convention if it conflicts with compassion and care for the people she meets. She is, or was for a time, a gay icon, especially in America, where her quirky British style and refusal to utter any word of condemnation of loving same-sex relationships won over people who often feel excluded from Christianity's embrace. As in Deadly Sins (page 109), she sensibly distinguishes in all her dealings with people between what is often perceived as "important" sin and the really destructive spiritual vices of cruelty and pride.

It is unusual to get any feedback from a television program, but the huge response to both her books and television appearances shows that Sister Wendy's thoughts on art have inspired and healed. This writer was privileged to be present when a woman stopped Sister Wendy in the middle of the Museum of Fine Arts in Boston and tearfully thanked her for the films that had helped her get through the deaths of both her husband and daughter in the same year. Wherever she goes there are plaudits and appeals for prayer that

Sister Wendy takes into her personal journey in the way she explains in Prayer Requests (page 67).

For those personal moments, if not for the dozens of television programs and twenty-two books she has produced, most of us would be happy to be remembered. Sister Wendy's ambition is predictably different:

> *I really don't want to be remembered, because I don't think I've done anything to be remembered for. I'd just like to die alone without the sisters anxiously clustering round me being kind and loving, and taking down final words. I'd like to be alone, and I'd like to be as much as possible forgotten. I can see nothing in myself to admire. I can see the greatness of God to admire; I wouldn't mind that being remembered: that God was so infinitely good to me, and right from the start, made me aware of what He was. But that could make people wish that they'd had that too, whereas He comes to them in a completely different way. No, I think best just to let me fall into the dust and go to Him.*

If Sister Wendy appears to have had two diametrically opposed careers, as a nun and an art critic, this book goes some way to unite them. There are art commentaries here, but these artworks are included not for their art historical importance, but because they have unique personal resonance in her spiritual life. This is a deeply intimate book, and the process of writing it has been more painful than many of her longer art books. And at a deeper level, it perhaps shows that one cannot define any vocation with a brand; lives are lived as a whole, not within the confines of any one job description. As Sister Wendy herself admits in Providence (page 62), sometimes the thing that "appears disastrous, the very thing we did *not* want, turns out to be a blessing."

In looking back over Sister Wendy's life, one can see a pattern that is close to a providential whole. Whether the young novice joined with full awareness or not, the active teaching order of Notre Dame produced the nun equipped to educate. The years of silence that followed in the camper seemed an end in themselves, but they not only gave Sister Wendy a unique capacity and knowledge of prayer, but also provided the freedom to look at and study art in a truly human way, unencumbered by the baggage of the art establishment. And in writing and talking about the art she had time to contemplate so deeply, the teacher reemerged for the wide audience she was perhaps always intended to reach.

Sister Wendy's success on television is undoubtedly due in part to the fact that she never talks down to the audience. There is no right and wrong in art. She merely invites the viewer to stand with her and share her appreciation of what she sees. When she was presenting on television, she made frequent requests to speak off camera: "It's not me that people want to see, but the art." These requests were always resisted by the director. But the careful viewer will notice that even when she is speaking on camera, for much of the time she is looking not at us, but at the painting. This book makes it clear that she applies exactly the same attitude to prayer. There are many insights here, but no definite, magic "answers." Sister Wendy is content simply to stand with us, facing in the same direction, toward God.

David Willcock is a television producer and writer. He and Sister Wendy have collaborated on eighteen television films at art galleries around the world. He is the coauthor with Tony Robinson of two history books, In Search of British Heroes *and* The Worst Jobs in History.

ONE

The Practice of Prayer

Do You Want to Pray?

One year — I forget the details — the Lenten sermons at Saint Patrick's in New York were given by a famous Jesuit who took prayer for his theme. He was much admired, but the compliment that stuck in his memory was that of an old priest who seemed to regard the very number and length of his sermons as constituting, per se, a sort of brilliant tour de force. "Because as you know, Father," he said, dropping his voice conspiratorially, "prayer's the simplest thing out." I hope the famous Jesuit did know, because the simplicity of prayer, its sheer, terrifying uncomplicatedness, seems to be the last thing most of us either know or want to know.

It is not difficult to intellectualize about prayer. Like love, beauty and motherhood, it quickly sets our eloquence aflow. It is not difficult, but it is perfectly futile. In fact, those glowing pages on prayer are worse than futile; they can be positively harmful. Writing about prayer, reading about prayer, talking about prayer, thinking about prayer, longing for prayer and wrapping myself more and more in these great cloudy sublimities can make me feel so aware of the spiritual — anything rather than actually praying. What am I doing but erecting a screen behind which I can safely maintain my self-esteem and hide away from God?

Ask yourself: what do I really want when I pray? Do you want to be possessed by God? Or to put the same question more honestly, do you want to want it? Then you have it. The one point Jesus stressed and repeated and brought up again is, "Whatever you ask the Father, He will grant it to you." His insistence on faith and perseverance are surely other ways of saying the same thing: you must really want, it must engross you. Wants that are passing, faint emotional desires that you do not press with burning conviction, these are things you do not ask "in Jesus' name"; how could you? But what you really want, "with all your heart and soul and mind and strength," that Jesus pledges himself to see that you are granted. He is not talking only, probably not even primarily, of prayer of petition, but of prayer. When you set yourself down to pray, *what do you want?* If you want God to take possession of you, then you are praying. That is all prayer is.

The astonishing thing about prayer is our inability to accept that if we have need of it, as we do, then because of

God's goodness, it cannot be something that is difficult. Accept that God is good and that your relationship with Him is prayer, and you must conclude that prayer is an act of the utmost simplicity. Yet so many people seem to feel that there is some mysterious method, some way in that others know, but they do not. "Knock and it shall be opened to you," but they seem to believe that it needs some sort of Masonic knock and their own humble tapping will go unnoticed. What kind of God thinks of tricks, lays down arcane rules, makes things difficult? God wants to love us and to give Himself. He wants to draw us to Himself, strengthen us, and infuse His peace. The humblest, most modest, almost imperceptible rubbing of our fingers on the door, and it flies open.

Prayer is the last thing we should feel discouraged about. It concerns nobody except God — always longing only to give Himself to us in love — and our own decision. And that, too, is God's, "who works in us to will and to effect." In a very true sense, there is nothing more to say about prayer, "the simplest thing out."

God's Business

Some artists seem to me, whether consciously or not, to use images that speak of the mystery of God. Craigie Aitchison is one. A favorite theme is the holy island of Lindisfarne seen across water, but here we feel the waters are not geographical (figure 1).

This boat sails on no specific sea, but on those mythic waters that have always been our image of the mysterious unknown of living. This is not an earthly sky, any more than this is an earthly sea. The small boat, its sail taut, does not reveal who is within it. Below our curious gaze, the sailor lies hidden. This boat that seemingly sails by itself can be seen to speak of prayer.

When we pray, we are likewise carried, borne along by a power that we do not and cannot direct. It is our prayer, our boat. It is we who have launched it on this sea of faith and we who stay quiet within it. But all the movement comes from God. We await Him, we surrender to Him. Where we want to go is not to the point; it is where God wants to take us. We do not see where that is. There is starlight, yes, but no sun or moon, no clarity of vision. Our world becomes duotone: scarlet sky, purple sea. All that is in our power is choice (as it is in life, which is meant to be prayer extended): do we stay still, hidden, unable to take control, or do we jump up and steer that boat ourselves, refusing God's lordship?

Put like that, it seems so obvious, yet it can be very hard to stay in this state of powerlessness, of blindness, of vulnerability accepted, when all that holds us motionless in the boat is our trust in God. But prayer is impossible without trust. We give our time and attention only and wholly because we believe that it is Jesus who prays within us. It is He who is united to His Father and we who live in

Him — and so with that divine Father. We may not feel that, or on the contrary, it may be the overwhelming certainty on which all we are is centered. Feeling or nonfeeling are equally unimportant. What matters is to stay at rest in the boat, down below sight level, while the wind that is the Holy Spirit bears us over the still waters to where the Father waits for us. "For the Son of God . . . was not Yes and No, but in him it is always Yes. For all the promises of God find their Yes in him" (2 Corinthians 1:19–20). *Boat* is the closest expression I have seen of making visual that sacred "Yes."

Your Unique Prayer

Prayer does not depend upon your natural capacity. What does depend upon your natural capacity is the kind of prayer, because it will be your prayer. But prayer itself is as simple as conversation between friends. No one would dare write a book on how husband and wife are to talk to each other — what topics are appropriate, what tone should be used — because obviously every marriage is different and goes through different phases. One of the responsibilities of any close relationship is that each person has to take seriously his or her need to talk, share, discuss and love. And this need will continually be changing. In prayer the relationship is between God and ourselves. God is always the same, but each of us is completely different.

The essential act of prayer is to stand unprotected before God. What will God do? He will take possession of us. That He should do this is the whole purpose of life. We know we belong to God; we know too, if we are honest, that almost despite ourselves, we keep a deathly hold on our own autonomy. We are willing, in fact very ready, to pay God lip service (just as we are ready to talk prayer rather than to pray), because waving God as a banner keeps our conscience quiet. But really to belong to God is another matter. It means having nothing left for ourselves, always bound to the will of Another, no sense of interior success to comfort us, living in the painful acknowledgement of being "unprofitable servants."

It is a terrible thing to be a fallen creature, and for most of the time we busily push this truth out of our awareness. But prayer places us helpless before God, and we taste the full bitterness of what we are. "Our God is a consuming fire," and my filth crackles as He seizes hold of me; He "is all light," and my darkness shrivels under His blaze. It is this naked blaze of God that makes prayer so terrible. For most of the time we can convince ourselves that we are good enough, good as the next man or woman — perhaps even better — who knows? Then we come to prayer — real prayer, unprotected prayer — and there is nothing left in us, no ground on which to stand.

Normally, as we grow older, we become progressively skilled in coping with life. In most departments, we acquire techniques on which we can fall back when interest and attention wilt. It is part of maturity that there is always some reserve we can tap. But this is not so in prayer. It is the only human activity that depends totally and solely on its intrinsic truth. We are there before God, or rather, to the degree that we are there before God, we are exposed to all that He is, and He can neither deceive nor be deceived. It is not that we want to deceive, whether God or anybody else, but with other people we cannot help our human condition of obscurity. We are not wholly there for them, nor they for us. We are simply not able to be so. Nor should we be. No human occasion calls for our total presence, even were it within our power to offer it. But prayer calls for it. Prayer is prayer if we want it to be.

Hunger for God

Saint Teresa of Avila, that great writer on prayer (a doctor of the Church solely because of what she said about prayer), never wearied of contemplating the story of Jesus and the Samaritan woman from Saint John's Gospel. It summed up for her what prayer was all about. And I am sorry that she would never have known far away in Spain of this great picture by Duccio, part of his masterwork for the cathedral in Siena (figure 2).

Duccio shows us an image of prayer, of the need and the hunger for God. The apostles have gone into the city to satisfy their hunger. They emerge in a compact bunch, supporting one another, protected from the clear light of

His presence by the fortress of the world, their own self-sufficiency.

Their hands are full, they clasp them to themselves, satisfied hands with the food of this world in their grasp. But the woman stands alone and exposed before Jesus. Her emptiness is seen not only in her hands, but in the most noticeable detail about her, which is the large empty pot on her head.

She does not hide her poor human emptiness: she exposes it, but the exposing is to Jesus. She is a living symbol of our need for Him. She stands still, an image of the stillness we choose at prayer. But Jesus does not reach out His hand to fill hers. He does not come to her. Jesus sits by the well and asks her to give to Him: her need is met with demand — again, a moving symbol of prayer. God gives Himself, not obviously, not in terms tangible or visible, but in holy contradiction. It is in giving that we receive: we, us. Our prayer may seem all nothingness, all *giving,* giving of time, of energy, of struggle to be present.

Jesus may seem to have only *asked,* not given. But that is how He does give. The woman went away, wholly changed, fed and renewed to her innermost depths. Yet she was given no water, no food. Jesus told her to draw her own water, and He revealed to her the shameful inner truth she carried. Yet this apparently merciless treatment was living water, was life, was communication of God at such intensity that there were no human terms in which the woman could see or judge what had happened to her. But she believed, and the whole city of her personality, her whole self, all she was and could become, believed with her.

Commonsense Prayer

When I first came to the camper, as part of the seven hours on my timetable, I got up in the middle of the night to pray for an hour. After a while I realized that this was sheer romanticism, because it really was not a very good time to pray. I was very sleepy in the middle of the night, and I often fell over in that hour of prayer. So I removed it to a less romantic but more fruitful time to pray.

Similarly, people often remark on my getting up early. I have found myself rising earlier and earlier. It used to be three o'clock. Now it is nearer to one in the morning, but this is not an act of self-denial. Going to bed early means I get up early. I have about seven and a half hours' sleep as a norm, which may be more than you, dear reader, have. Depriving oneself of sleep seems to me a kind of penance that does not accept the reality of being flesh and blood. We need sleep. That is the way we are made. Not sybaritic sleep, too much of it, but enough sleep to fit us for the day ahead.

We are told in the Gospels that Jesus got up very early in the morning to pray. This was a practical decision: very early in the morning was the one time when He knew He would not be disturbed. I decided when I came to live alone that I would have the same simple meal every day and wear the same simple habit. My intention was to liberate myself from having to think about cooking or menus or choice of clothes. This simplification has worked very well for me. This is a world away from the austerities of Celtic saints like Saint Cuthbert, immersing themselves in freezing water and staying awake almost for the sake of being awake. It has always seemed to me that austerity should be functional. It is a way of simplifying our lives, setting us free to adhere to God and God alone.

Prayer in Everyday Life

Everybody reading this book has his or her own vocation and his or her own life.

Perhaps you have a baby? Perhaps you have an especially demanding workload? Perhaps you are lonely? Perhaps you are angry? None of this matters. It is who you are that God comes to in prayer, and if it is a tired, fractious, despondent man or woman, He still takes you to Himself with infinite love and makes the best of what you can give Him. Your life is not my life. I long to use what has happened and is happening to me as a place where God can reveal His love. My regime, my life, may sound more romantic, more spiritual than yours, but yours is equally valid, equally a place for God to reveal Himself. Crying baby, difficult boss, the pressures of the mortgage, all the horrors of the workplace — none of these are invalidating; they just make part of the reality that is you, and it is only to this reality that God can respond.

What matters is that whatever your circumstances, however helpful (like mine) or unhelpful (I hope not like yours), we retain possession of our selfhood and offer it to God. It is the offering that matters, the will, the choosing. If your life is difficult, it could well be that you are more open to God than someone like myself whose life has been so sheltered.

Sometimes people have told me, "I felt too sick to pray." If you think about it, this is really saying, "God cannot come to the sick." What is meant is, "I feel too sick to feel I am praying," or "I feel too worried to feel I am praying. How can I pray when all I can think about is my coming operation?" This misunderstands the essence of prayer, which is God's business. You bring yourself in whatever state you are and offer that to God. There may be very little satisfaction in this. All you may be conscious of are your own feelings, miserable and inadequate, but God does not ask us to pass a test of how beautiful our feelings are. He simply wants us to want to pray.

What Should I Do?

It is one of the most frequently asked questions: what should I do during prayer? How eagerly people long to be told the answer! For that would make me safe, well protected: I would know what to do! But the answer is of the usual appalling simplicity: stand before God unprotected, and you will know yourself what to do. I mean this in utter earnest. Methods are of value, naturally, but only as something to do "if I want to," which in this context of response to God means "if he wants me to." I may feel drawn to meditate, to sing to Him, or to stay before Him in, say, an attitude of contrition or praise.

But we cannot say prayers at all unless we know also the prayer of silence. In silent prayer there are no words and hence no thoughts. We are still. This silence is nothing to be afraid of. Five or ten minutes, whatever can be spared. You are just there to stand in His presence and let Him take possession of you.

Whether you are aware of that presence does not matter. God is there, whatever your feelings, just as Jesus knew God was there even when He felt abandoned on the cross. What pure praise of the Father's love; to feel abandoned and yet stay content before Him, saying, "Father, into your hands . . ." We cannot sufficiently emphasize to ourselves that prayer is God's concern, and His one desire is "to come and make His abode with us." Do we believe Him or not? Of course, I can cheat. If I choose not to be there for Him (and since I am not yet transformed into Jesus, to some extent I always do protect myself against the impact of His love), then that is cause for grief. But it is creative grief. It drives us helpless to Jesus to be healed. We say to Him: "If you want to, you can make me clean." But He answers, "I do want to — but do you?" That wanting is ever the crux of the matter.

Silence

There is a tendency today for people to say, with greater or less distress, that they have no time for prayer. What they mean is, they do not have a peaceful hour, or two peaceful half hours, or even three peaceful twenty minutes. If that is the day God has given them, then He awaits their praying hearts under precisely these conditions. They are testing conditions, surely, but never impossible. Most of us can manage a ten-minute silence. It may have to be in the lavatory, or the bath, or the car, or standing at the station, or when the baby's just gone to sleep. But for most people it is possible. If you can spend it sitting quietly, I rejoice for you. But this concentrated time when you try to put aside all else and simply be there for God is the proof, as it were, of your desire to pray.

Take these times, poor crumbs of minutes though they be, and give yourself to God in them. You will not be able to feel prayerful in them, but that is beside the point. You pray for God's sake, you are there for Him to look on you, to love you, to take His holy pleasure in you. What can it matter whether you feel any of this or get any comfort from it? We should be misers in prayer, scraping up these flinders of time and holding them out trustfully to the Father. But we should also watch out for the longer stretches we may be missing because we do not want to see them. Many things that are pleasant and profitable — television programs, books, conversations — may have to be sacrificed at times. But you will make this and any other sacrifice if you hunger and thirst for God to possess you, and this is my whole point. There is time enough for what matters supremely to us, and there always will be.

Silence II

It might seem rather paradoxical to take a musician as an image of silence, but what I have always found so beautiful about Gentileschi's lute player is her attitude of listening (figure 3). Is she making music, or is she hearing it in her mind? That voluminous white sleeve, such a glorious contrast to the mustard yellow of her gown, seems to obscure the musical score. Yet her face is expressive of such inner awareness. It is a remarkably still painting; the young girl as still as the musical still life that is spread out on the table. She is a human still life, life seen as still, as silent as it is in true prayer. Add a halo, and we would think we had a Saint Cecilia, patron saint of music. But Gentileschi is touchingly concerned to depict a very ordinary, unglamorous young woman alone and absorbed by the power of music. The poet John Donne, roughly contemporary with Gentileschi, prays that at death we will "become His music," and there has always been a subliminal correspondence between the spirituality of music and that of prayer. Music is a kind of prayer, a very real one, just as are poetry and art. Go further: if we truly seek God, everything is prayer to us.

Perhaps the most underestimated virtue is that of spiritual awareness, which used to be called "recollection." This is precisely what we see in *The Lute Player*, a listening, an attentiveness, the condition in which God can give Himself to us.

Prayer Will Never Get in the Way

You can be quite certain that your desire to pray will never interfere with your obligations. It cannot. Your responsibilities are part of you, and it is this real, burdened, perhaps even overburdened person whom God loves and in whom he believes. The temptation always is to think that religion means we must be different, unencumbered by the world. This is not so. Look at the life of Jesus. He lived in a quarrelsome, demanding, hostile world and accepted all of it as the world His Father would redeem.

Prayer and Wholeness

God wants you to be the fullness of what you can be. You cannot become this if you do not allow Him to enter into you. You do your feeble search for Him, and He will do His mighty search for you. "Seek and ye shall find." The "you" God seeks may not be the "you" of whom you are aware. It is the essential you, the real you, the fullness of your potential. The transformation from one to the other, the realizing of that potential you, may take a lifetime. Few of us will ever wholly achieve this complete surrender. But all God needs is your desire.

If you do not let God start the process of taking this real you to Himself, you will always be stunted. God grieves that you will never be His beautiful adult child because you refuse to let yourself be. We all know parents who have seen their child fritter away his or her gifts, take drugs, make a foolish, destructive marriage. God feels this infinitely more, because His love for you is far deeper and more constructive than the most loving of parents can feel for their child. God is both conceptually apart from us and really within us: in God we live and move and have our being. It is an extraordinary statement that "in God we have our being." It is absolutely true. That we have no idea what it means does not make it any less true. The only one who knew what it meant was Jesus. He alone knew what it meant to live every moment in the absolute consciousness of His Father's love. We cannot know like Jesus, but in faith, in trust, we, too, can share in that intimacy by joining ourselves to Christ. As Christians we live in His faith and His love.

Concentration

In the Eastern Church the feast of the Epiphany, perhaps the greatest in the liturgical year, celebrates not so much the coming of the Magi to Bethlehem as the epiphany that Jesus Himself experienced at His baptism in the Jordan (figure 4). This was surely the climactic revelation of Jesus' life. It was here, standing humbly in the water, with John the Baptist baptizing Him as he did all those who came in penitence, that the Father and the Holy Spirit revealed themselves to Jesus. A voice was heard from heaven, "Thou art my beloved Son: with thee I am well pleased." And over His head, hovering in the form of a dove, was the Holy Spirit.

What moves me so profoundly about this image is the total concentration of Jesus. He is completely alone, John tensely pouring the water on one side and the angelic trio looking on in languid amazement on the other. Even the water has withdrawn from His feet. Piero is honoring an old legend that the Jordan felt unworthy of the presence of Jesus. Jesus is totally folded in on Himself, aware only of the Father and the Father's love, and its significance. This is what we long to be in prayer: one who is utterly given, stretching out beyond the immediate to the absolute reality of God.

It is a magnificent picture, with the strong white column of Jesus' body paralleled by the strong white trunk of the young tree, while behind the rough poetry of the whole material world waits to be given meaning. Jesus is its meaning, and it is at this moment He realizes that this is His vocation, to reveal the beauty and the truth and the love of His Father. It is His vocation to rescue the world from incoherence. We intuit this because we have studied the Scriptures, but there are no emotions on that grave and youthful face, only the seriousness of total concentration.

Our Father

When Jesus was asked by the apostles to teach them how to pray, He did not tell them to do as He did, which was apparently to go into a lonely place and be still. Rather, He gave them words—the Our Father—which spell out in very simple terms the attitudes that we should bring to prayer. We say the Our Father, and so we should, but it is the desires behind the words that make this prayer so significant.

Books have been written on the implications of what Jesus said. Take even the first words, that we call God "Father" and that we call Him "our"—Father of us all. If these two words are understood, all divisions between peoples are seen as false and so too is any idea of God as judge or stern taskmaster. Meditating on these words, even just these two, takes us deep into the mystery that Jesus understood and longed to share with us.

The more we have pondered on our faith, which comes to us in words, the more we bring to prayer a spirit aware and alive. Rote prayer is not prayer at all. It is impossible to overemphasize the importance of bringing to prayer the absolute truth of what we are and what God desires us to be. If we have never bothered to understand our faith, to read about it, to discuss it, then it is that uninterested person who comes to pray. Whatever we may like to think, how can we be giving real attention to God in prayer when for the rest of the time He seems to matter so little?

Now, consider the other petitions. Jesus gives as the first thing to be prayed for that His Father's name should be hallowed, that God should be revered, that what God is should matter to us all. Hallow God's name, and wars die away, malice and hatred have no place. More wars have been launched "in the name of God" than for any other reason, and the same is true of interreligious hatred, but this is not in the name of God "our Father." It is in the name of a man-made God who hates and destroys, never the God of Jesus.

When we go on to say "Thy kingdom come," it is the kingdom of our Father, a world ruled by love and understanding. This is the happy world for which we were made, and for which we pray. It is a happy world because here His will is done, and if we have understood the meaning of "our" and "Father," we will know that this will is for our fullness of being. Jesus spoke of it as life, "life to the full."

Living like this in the Father's world does not come easily, and so we pray for our daily bread: nourishment, perhaps material — we all need to eat — but certainly spiritual. Our wills need sustaining in the very demanding task of loving one another. We can be foolishly held back by a sense of guilt, and so we ask to have our trespasses forgiven. We ask with confidence because forgiving is natural to God, not something to be coaxed out of Him with prayer and sacrifice. There is a condition, though — not one imposed by God, but one intrinsic to being human. Forgive us . . . as we forgive those who trespass against us. The point is, we cannot receive God's forgiveness if we are too stubborn to forgive ourselves. Forgiveness, as it were, bounces off a hard heart. Making the effort to forgive another person opens us up to receive forgiveness for ourselves.

Weak, daft creatures that we are, we ask God to temper the wind to His shorn lambs, "lead us not into temptation, but deliver us from evil." It is not that God "leads," but that this is the Hebrew manner of asking to have temptation kept away from us. Should it come, though, we trust that He will deliver us. After all, the holy name Jesus means Savior, Deliverer, He Who Rescues Us. From what are we rescued? It is from that innate nastiness of which we are all aware. We come to be true children of "our Father" by trying to be and by praying to be.

Levels of Prayer

Prayer is essentially an attitude. We trust God, we believe in Him, we turn to Him. An attitude is something permanent. So how could prayer stop when we, as it were, stop praying? It would be as if your relationship with your parents existed only when you were in actual contact with them.

I think there are different levels of prayer. The deepest level is that wordless union with God that is indescribable. There is nothing to say about this, because there are no concepts that one can get hold of to talk about what happens. My guess would be that we all know this level, even in the most fleeting form. Has everybody not experienced a moment when beauty or wonder touched them at depth? Because this touch of God escapes all the confines of the human mind, there is literally nothing more to be said about it.

Then there is the level that would fit more comfortably into what most people think of as prayer. We are in church, or we are on our knees, and we are, as the catechism says, "directing the mind and heart to God." We know what we are doing: we are praying. Most commonly we are petitioning, but also we can be glorying, or thanking, or simply telling God how we feel. (Telling God that you have a cold and are greatly tempted to impatience is perfectly valid prayer.) All church services are structured on this level of prayer. And so are meditation books. Also when we sit down to think about a passage in the Scriptures and to ponder its meanings for us. The defining note of this broad and vital level of prayer is that we use words, either vocally or mentally.

A less structured level is what I would call spiritual talk. Here you are not directly addressing God, but are engaged in the mystery of what He is. Listening to sermons comes into this level. Saint Teresa of Avila said she had never heard a sermon so bad she could not get something from it (I suppose even compassion for the preacher). Even more, talking to friends about the things of God comes into this layer. Parents teaching their children about God comes here, and schoolteachers trying to share with their pupils a sense of God's wonder and of the actual nature of faith. All these occupations make sense only because we want to love God. In their own way they are an expression of that love and a means of deepening it.

There are, obviously, large parts of the day, most of it in fact, where none of these activities are taking place: our working day. We do not sanctify our normal activities by interspersing them with pious thoughts. Work demands as its right our full concentration, and so does much else in the day. God's good food — surely we should appreciate it and take time to do so. The companionship of friends and all that makes leisure pleasurable: these are things to be enjoyed and savored, not rushed through as not truly spiritual. Jesus shocked the pious of His day by His delight in rather raffish company. He was criticized as a "glutton and a wine-bibber," only, as far as one can see, because He had a healthy enjoyment of what it means to be human. Yet how can we doubt that at every moment Jesus was intimately united with His Father? Providing wine for the wedding guests at Cana was as sacramental for Him as feeding the apostles with His body and blood at the Last Supper. All life is holy. If we are truly oriented toward God, then our slightest activities — shaving, reading the newspaper, putting out the cat — are a form of prayer.

One might call this the lowest level of prayer and, of itself, it will not sustain us. But then it is not expected to. An attitude that seeks God as primary reality will always move deeper and deeper to the heart of prayer. What love could be satisfied with peripheral contact? Love will always seek to come closer and closer, so paradoxically the lowest level of prayer is not possible without the higher. "Love me and do what you will." Because if you love, you will always be held in the nexus of that love, and you will never will anything that denies it.

Perseverance

In an article titled "Criticism After Art" in the *New Criterion* magazine, James Pinero has this to say: "A world of difference separates those who criticize art from those who seek to know how art criticism is done, because art criticism is done by doing it."

Perhaps of all the advice one can receive about prayer, this is the most crucial. We learn to pray by praying. What Pinero does not explicitly mention is that the art critic obviously improves the more seriously and assiduously he practices his profession. Another critic, asked portentously how he set about his task, merely said he looked at art and wrote about it. One who prays could say the same. We look at God and live out in practice the grace He has given us.

We have to start somewhere, and looking—for an art critic and, still more, for the one who wants to pray—is by no means easy. It will become easy or, at least, easier, in time. If we persevere long enough, it may even become instinctive, the way we function, but it does not start like that. It starts with making resolutions, imposing order when we might like the pleasure of disorder, doing whatever is necessary to align ourselves with God. It may take years before we have the habit of prayer, as it were. But if we want it, we will most certainly be given it. If we do our bit to persevere, God will never let us down. He will always ensure that we have the capacity for the prayer we desire. In the end, it is God's faithfulness that is the issue, far more than our own.

Trust

Abraham believed that God was calling him to sacrifice Isaac, his only son. The Bible spells out his predicament in all its terrible detail. He loads up the boy with the material for the sacrifice, and when Isaac, puzzled, asks where the sacrifice is, his father can only reply, "God will provide." It is an excruciating story of a moral dilemma. Isaac loves his father and trusts him. Abraham loves God and trusts Him. He lays his son upon the stone and raises the knife. Still the boy trusts his father. Still the man trusts his God. Yet, we ask, how could Abraham have thought that God would demand human sacrifice? All the movement of the Old

Testament is away from the murderous cultic acts that distinguish the pagans, moving nearer and nearer to the moral purity that is the essence of God. How ambivalent Abraham must have felt, how uncertain. We, as outsiders, can see that he was subjectively in error. God could never have demanded this, even as a test. At some level Abraham surely knew this; at another level, blinded by his imagination into believing that God was making these terrible demands, he pressed on.

Chagall enters fully into the horror of the situation (figure 5). Abraham's eyes are closed as he hefts a knife in one hand and the flame for the sacrifice in the other. Isaac crosses his arms in obedience, still, we feel certain, believing in his father's love, as we know the story has a happy ending. God sends an angel to hold back the sacrificing knife and provides a ram caught in the thicket as a substitute. What I find so poignant here is the absoluteness with which we can depend upon God. However mistaken our ideas, even if we imagine we have revelations, God will always save us from our mistakes. He saves us in prayer. Take to prayer, whatever your beliefs and disbeliefs, and you can be as confident as Abraham and Isaac that God will make the truth plain to you.

Truth is infinitely dear to God. It is the one virtue with which His Son identified Himself: "I am the Truth." Trying to live the truth in our daily life, and clinging to Jesus, the Truth, in our prayer, we shall always be safeguarded.

The Name of Jesus

If I had to suggest one prayer—we are talking of words here—that will always strengthen us and bring us peace, I would offer simply the word "Jesus." For years I found it impossible actually to say this name except in a ritualized context of vocal prayer. A name is so intensely personal. It is us in shorthand, but the whole us.

Scripture tells us that one of the great joys of entering heaven will be that God will call us by our name. In fact, God is the only one who really knows our name, the full dimensions of our name, because it is only He who knows us absolutely. We do not even know ourselves (but sometimes make unpleasant discoveries). But God knows us through and through; all of us, good and bad.

This sense of name becomes overwhelming when we think of our Lord. When we say "Jesus," we literally do not know what we say. We are pronouncing the fullness of Godhead and manhood united—who can understand that? Yet it has always seemed to me that there is an enormous tenderness in calling on someone we love by name. Think of Mary Magdalene in the garden on the day of resurrection. She does not recognize Jesus, and it is only when He calls her Mary that her eyes are opened.

We will have to wait for heaven to hear God call our name, but here on earth at any moment we can call upon His. It always seems to me the most daring, trustful and extraordinary of privileges that any one of us can actually address Christ by His intimate name. When my father was dying, I found myself alone with him except, of course, for the medical staff. One of the nurses urged me to speak to him. This was the culminating moment of my father's life. I could think of nothing that would not trivialize it, even to tell him that I loved him. I could see too that all his endeavor was set upon God. The only word that seemed to me adequate in such a sacred moment was the holy name of Jesus. Holding his dying hand, and saying again and again that name, I realized that my father and I were sharing the same spiritual space.

Does Prayer Work?

Almost invariably when one talks about prayer, people think it is about asking God for something. Whenever we turn to God, we are praying, and I suppose that the most frequent motive for this turning is that we want something. But how disheartening to read in autobiographies or to hear from people that they lost their faith when they prayed very earnestly to God and nothing happened. What is disheartening is that we have here a misunderstanding of the prayer of petition.

It may seem to us that we are asking God to give us something—good weather, good health, good exam results—and, of course, that is our explicit intention. Since God is not a puppeteer who will stretch out and change the weather, adjust the cells of our body, or jiggle with the examiner's markings (and at a deeper level we know this), the essential nature of our plea is not that God will change the real world, but that he will strengthen us to bear the impact of it.

Disappointment and misfortune, humiliation, pain and tragedy are all extremely difficult to endure. We need help to take what comes and grow through it, by means of it. Good fortune, too — getting what we want — has its dangers. We can become overconfident, we can live carelessly and foolishly. Asking God's help protects us against all consequences, and it is this safety and freedom that we will always receive when we turn to God in prayer.

Yet somehow, human nature being what it is, with our ingrained desire for miraculous solutions and retrievals, we find the nature of God's help unsatisfying. Notice how whenever there is a disaster, people look around to find who is to blame and rage against the inadequacy of official support.

Perhaps, ironically, one of the strongest arguments *for* the existence of God is this deep-rooted sense of injustice, a sense that we are not on our own; and if we are not on our own, then we have a right to be helped. To be left sitting in our misery, our homes destroyed by the tsunami — how can we reconcile this with a loving and all-powerful Father? Or to have the widespread destruction of people and livelihoods that follows a terrorist attack — is this truly consistent with what our faith tells us of God? In a way it would be easier to say that it is not and to become atheists. But if it is not, it is because we are reading the situation wrong.

Having God as our Father does not relegate us to the position of perpetual children. Children do expect that their parents will put things right, and it can be a shattering experience to realize that parents are weak and human. But from the shards we build up a more adult personality. Bad things happen, sometimes for no apparent reason. We have to accept them and grow through them and never let them damage us. They will wound us, yes, but damage is another matter, and that is precisely what prayer guards against.

Life is unpredictable. Tragedy and comedy come down upon us without warning. This may be part of the fascination of playing or watching sport. The ball always comes from an angle the player could not anticipate, and the skill is all in the reaction. In real life the same is true. How do we react? When do we feel it right to take the initiative, and if we do, what kind? Pure passive endurance can never be the whole answer. It is in coping with this, the strangeness and stresses of even a normal day, that we need the help of God. We would like Him to change these stresses. This will not happen. What will happen is His support in making everything in our lives a means of deepening our capacity to be human. Not God the puppeteer, pulling the strings for His favorites, but the God who has resolutely refused to people His world with puppets. He has paid us the compliment of creating us as free and intelligent, able to choose and reject and look clearly at the truth.

Providence

It is natural enough that we should pray for what we want, always keeping in mind that the real meaning of any petition is to be given grace to accept what happens. Sometimes we can see for ourselves that what appears disastrous, the very thing we did *not* want, turns out to be a blessing. For example, I would never have chosen to leave my solitude to work in television. I did it because it seemed right. If I had something to share with people, it would be selfish to refuse. Although there were many pleasant aspects of the work, it seemed to me I was making a sacrifice. Yet I gained enormously from this unwillingly shouldered burden. The people I met in the television world taught me so much about God. I was shamed by their earnestness, their hard work, their desire to do the best job possible. Although, like an onion, I have still many skins of selfishness, quite a few were peeled away in the purification of this exposure.

I am sure everyone who is reading this book can match such a discovery. It is not that reality conforms itself to our needs, but that we learn how to conform ourselves to what reality is offering. What I call Providence is always there in wait, as it were. What prayer does is alert us to its presence so that we are always making the best of things and not the worst. Tragedy and frustration remain their painful selves, but prayer in accepting them changes the pain into something redemptive.

Suffering

Probably the absolute in suffering is the Holocaust. The memory of it overshadows all our reflections. That this horror actually happened — who can explain it? For lovers of God, who can explain it away? We are told that a rabbi in Auschwitz cried out plaintively to God, "Where are you, Lord?" His answer was "I am with you. I, too, am in Auschwitz." This is faith at its most absolute. This is the faith that cries out, in the words of the King James Bible, "Though he slay me, yet will I trust Him" (Job 13:15). It is a faith that transcends experiences and clings to the reality of what God is.

For Christians (and this is the same God as that of the rabbi), the God who accepted being crucified — Jesus on the cross — accepted crucifixion because He saw what would become of it. It would redeem the world because it would offer people a faith that would change their lives. But it is we who have to change our lives. God will never do it for us. He showed us that on the cross. He suffers with us. He suffers in us. He makes suffering bearable.

God never sends suffering. Never. It is never "God's will" that we should suffer. God would like us not to suffer. But since the world brings suffering, and since God refuses to use His almighty power and treat us as foolish children,

He aligns Himself with us, goes into Auschwitz with us, is devastated by 9/11 with us, and draws us with Him through it all into fulfillment. This is a high price to pay for our human freedom, but it is worth it. To be mere automatons for whom God arranges the world to cause us no suffering would mean we never have a self. We could not make choices. It would mean that you could not choose your own boyfriend or girlfriend, because you would be pro-grammed to take the one who would make you happiest or the one who would make you most virtuous. If you are not programmed, you live in a world of choices and one per-son's choice may mean suffering for another. In theory, we could live without causing pain to others, but in real life all human beings are vulnerable. We can never become fully human if we are protected from life. We have to learn and understand our vulnerability.

This is extremely painful. Deep down in our subcon-scious lurks the thought that if I could control my own life, I would do much better. This is one of the great insights of prayer: our lives are not in our control. We are like batters at cricket or baseball: fast or slow, spinning or curving, we have to deal with the ball as it comes. We are like tennis players: if they could control how the ball crossed the net, they would win all their matches. No, life is an infinitely complex thing, and we have to accept that we are adults, which we hate, and we have responsibility, which we would like to put onto God, but God is not going to take that away from us. What He will do, as we pray, is to be with us in it all, swinging the bat with us, lifting the racket with us, sharing both triumph and disaster.

Suffering II

The most powerful visual expression of faith and suffering that I know is Tiepolo's *Martyrdom of Saint Agatha* (figure 6).

Great though he is, Tiepolo is not a spiritual heavyweight like Rembrandt or Rothko. He is essentially a superb decorator, floating on the princely and ecclesiastical ceilings his lovely and gracious images, in which everybody is beautiful, and even disaster is elegant. Yet I turn frequently and humbly to his great *Saint Agatha*.

This saint had a particularly awful martyrdom: her breasts were cut off. I can remember as a child reading about Saint Agatha in Butler's *Lives of the Saints*, and closing the book with a sickened awareness of what complete faith might entail. She was a popular saint for centuries, but the images of her were delightfully anodyne: she looked radiant and carried a plate on which reposed two small pink mounds. Here is martyrdom made painless. But Tiepolo, however devout, was an eighteenth-century realist when it came to martyrdom, and this painting spares us nothing. We are confronted with a real woman, bleeding painfully to death. She is not alone: the executioner looms behind her, a grieving friend holds a cloth to her bosom, a detached page carries away her breasts, but they are merely background. Our attention is riveted by the dying saint, already almost bloodless, eyes swollen with tears. She holds out her hands and looks upward. It is this look that so moves me. Clearly she looks up to God, but not in hope: she does not expect salvation in any physical sense. Nor does she look with reproach, as if God had not answered her prayers.

It is a look hard to decipher, but I would say it is basically a look of agonized trust. In shock over the horror of what has been done to her, fading out of life, she still tells us with every aspect of her body that she knows God is with her. He answers her prayer by suffering within her, making the insupportable possible. She feels only death and pain, but her inner self, that which makes her who she is, cleaves to God with childlike confidence. Tiepolo gives us no easy answers, no escapes from the harshness of life. But this painting shows visually what it means to have faith.

When I went to film in Berlin, the Gemäldegalerie allowed us to film only at night, when the visitors and cleaners had gone. I had chosen to speak only about German painters, but I longed to see the Tiepolo. But when I asked, I was told that it was in a distant gallery, where the electricity had been switched off. The two middle-aged guards — both had very lived-in faces, which made one aware of what Berlin had suffered — said they would take me while the cameras were being set up. We set off with flashlights, along dark corridors and up mysterious stairs, until we came to where *Saint Agatha* was on view. So I saw her, more or less alone, by flashlight, in a deep silence. It was an unforgettable privilege.

Prayer Requests

What happens when people ask us to pray for them? Perhaps I can tell you only what happens within me. I have heard the request, and hearing it has changed me. I am now a person who knows that X wants a baby, that Y is sick, that Z is locked in an unhappy marriage. I say, "Yes, I will pray for you," and I mean it. But what I mean is that this person, this me, who now has this knowledge, gives herself to God and, in the giving, I give all these problems. None of them are new to God. He knows far better than I can ever know what longing and anguish lie behind every request, but these requests are now part of me. I do not verbalize them, I may never even think of them specifically, but I am confident that I have given them to God, and He thinks about them and longs to support my friends with his strength and understanding. God knows much more about the joys and sorrows of humanity than any of us could ever do. So when He takes possession, He takes possession with all that He sees and knows, and I am content with that.

It seems to me that everybody I have ever met, whether I remember them distinctly or not, is now part of my journey. This is true of you also. Your family, your friends, those you know at work or elsewhere—all who have impinged upon you have become involved in your journey toward God. In a rather alarming sense, to know someone is to be responsible for them. These people are your neighbors. And God judges us on how we have loved our neighbor. There is no prayer that does not affect our life. We are a unit, a whole, and we cannot spin off prayer and make it distinct from life.

TWO

Prayer and Belief

Do You Need Organized Religion?

If you are reading this book, I presume that you are somebody who wants to pray. But do you need to belong to a religion in order to pray? I can say only that this is up to you. A religion is a means to an end. In itself it is not an end, but of value only if it takes us to God, serving as a springboard.

It is, however, a very good springboard. And I am speaking now of the true religion that understands the beauty and tenderness of God and helps us to respond to Him. If you like, think of religion as a trellis, a framework, on which the vine of love can grow. I have met people who have not found within themselves the need for a religion and yet are giving God infinitely more praise than somebody "devoutly religious" whose religion is not a springboard but a camping site. Such people are rare, however.

Most of us need the support of religion, and it would be presumptuous to discard the structure it can give to our capacity to love God. For myself this is certainly true. I need the support of religion. With its help I soar free.

The Sacrament

All religions are based upon prayer, on a true, living contact with the living God. Nothing could express the wonder of God's embrace more beautifully than the writings of the medieval Sufi mystics of Islam. For me, the religion that supports me in an attitude of surrender is Catholicism. And the greatest empowerment that it offers is the holy mass.

This is for me the prime source of infused energy. The mass is the work of Jesus, his Last Supper made actual. In it, it seems that we plug into the divine energy and are lifted out of the pettiness of self into the infinite love of the Son for His Father.

You may have read spiritual books that describe ecstasies and visions. These seem to me almost shadowy compared to the reality of what happens at mass. At the Last Supper, Jesus gave Himself to be consumed, to be eaten under the form of bread and wine. When the Last Supper is renewed in the mass, He gives Himself all over again. He takes with Him those who join in the Eucharist. Lifted out of your own smallness into something inconceivably vast, the self-giving of Jesus, you then have His gift sealed, as it were, through Holy Communion.

Whatever your religion, if you pray, you want to be taken up into God and used for the world. No gift from God is just for ourselves. It is always for using, for other people. This is what the consecration — the priest raising the bread and wine and declaring "This is my body, this is my blood" — makes visual. God continually gives Himself to us so that we may give ourselves to others. It actualizes our desire to receive God and to give God so that we can live the day not in our own strength, but in His.

Even for Catholics, the Eucharist is something mysterious. It is both sacrifice and celebration, a spiritual reenactment of the Last Supper. Medieval theologians made up a word for what happens and called it "transubstantiation." This means that materially, physically, the bread and wine are still there, but in actuality the essence of them has been changed into the true living body of Christ. The center of the mass is the consecration when this mystical change happens, and the climax is when those who are sharing in the sacrifice receive Holy Communion. I love what C. S. Lewis said, that we are told to "take and eat" not "take and understand." None of us can "understand" — the mystery is beyond our comprehension, but I am certain that something profoundly real happens at mass.

Mass is, after all, essentially a form of prayer, the highest form, and emotions will always be peripheral. What happens does not depend on our feelings or the devotion with which the priest says mass. It depends simply and only on faith and the choice we make to surrender ourselves to

Jesus. This is His business, His mass. The priest is the stand-in for the Lord. In that offering, that consecration, that giving, we are taken into Jesus and set free in a way that is impossible to describe.

Because this gift is so freely given, there is a danger that we take it for granted. I think if mass were rationed, if it were said once a decade or even perhaps only once a year, people would come trembling and in awe to be lifted out and up into Jesus and given to the Father, totally given to the Father for the world that He loves.

The Passion of Christ

When I speak about the mass, I know that I am speaking under a different form about the Crucifixion. The Last Supper reached its necessary fulfillment on the cross. But because the mass is bloodless — the imagery is of bread and wine — I do not have to face that which I find so painful, the physical actualities of the death of Jesus.

Because I find this so moving, it would have been very difficult to speak about it, but for me this difficulty is magnified almost indefinitely by any image that depicts the Passion of Christ. I fully admit this is a personal defect, a weakness, even a cowardice, but I cannot look on a picture of Jesus, whom I so love, in His death agonies. I can force myself ("He suffered it; you can at least look"), but the strain means that it is beyond my abilities to look and, as well, respond to the art as art. This means, I am sorry to confess, that I go around the great galleries of the world, scurrying hastily past some of their greatest paintings: Rubens' *The Descent from the Cross*, Titian's *Burial*, Grünewald's *Crucifixion*. I can look but not dwell, not really allow the painting to speak to me. You will understand, then, with what relief and joy I came upon, at the Getty in Los Angeles, an image of the dying Lord that I can indeed contemplate and stay with and let impose itself. It is El Greco's *Christ on the Cross*, an image of which there are several examples (figure 7). He was a thrifty artist; once El Greco created an image he liked, he took great pleasure in repeating it. He shows Jesus, with his naked body long, slender and gleaming with light as He opens His arms on the cross. He is alone. Behind Him surge black clouds, shot through here and there by a brilliant light. But it is as if all the brightness in this dark and tragic world comes from Jesus. We can dimly see behind and below Him the pale bones of other victims, and in the distance men on horseback, waving banners, set off toward a fortified city. The world is leaving Him. Yet Jesus is triumphant, not despite His wounds and crown of thorns, but because of them, through them. He rises. In death He expresses the Resurrection. Jesus did truly die, but He went into death and out of it into glory. Somehow El Greco makes visible both aspects of the Crucifixion, what it was in itself and what it was mystically. Time separates "Christ has died" from "Christ is risen"; we move through one to the other. But here we have both together, each given full weight. If I can look at Jesus in His Passion and at the same time see Him in His glory, I have no need to flinch. This is what the agony meant, that He would soar into the freedom of the Spirit. Everything in this painting draws me closer to God, to the silence that is prayer.

The Scriptures

Our deepest knowledge of Jesus comes from prayer. There He takes possession of us and shows us what He is. But this is not a tangible, visual or conceptual knowledge. And it needs an intellectual understanding on our part for this silent awareness to become vitalized (that is, show itself in works of love).

How can we say we love God if we ignore His own revelation of Himself in the Scriptures? If we take prayer seriously, we must take spiritual reading seriously, and the essential reading will always be the Bible. Let me add immediately that we need the Bible with commentaries. Of itself the Word of God can be perplexing. Scholars can explain to us the thought patterns of the past, the true meanings of words that have changed over the centuries. Obviously there are many scholars and many varieties of commentaries, but I think we can tell when what is said comes from the writer's own prayer and so deepens our prayer. Reading Scripture, thinking about Scripture, studying Scripture, meditating Scripture — these are essential preludes to the silent acceptance of the reality of God in prayer.

In one sense Scripture is all-important. In another sense it is dangerous by itself, because these are very ancient texts and no amount of goodwill can ensure that we truly understand them. If we need to be assiduous in our reading of Scripture, we also need to be humble. Remember what Saint Peter says in his second letter: "There are some things in them hard to understand, which the ignorant and unstable twist to their destruction" (2 Peter 3:16). In other words, beware if you have an agenda. God will reflect Himself in the still surface of a pure heart, and the humble labor of searching through Scripture commentaries helps to keep our heart simple.

After Scripture and Scripture commentaries, I think we should read books that draw us closer to God (I am hoping with all my heart that the book you are reading will be one such). I am not just thinking of lives of the saints or histories of the Church, but of all those books that show human goodness and courage. I myself find books about mountaineering deeply inspiring, or books about the courage of early explorers, or of any who have subsumed their earthly longings into a desire to excel at some art or physical skill: ballet dancers, ice-skaters, violinists. How they urge me to set my gaze wholly on God and ignore the cost!

To Pray Is to Be Alive

Talking about things instead of doing them is very dangerous. This is the difficulty about a book on prayer. The more
we talk about prayer and write about prayer, the more we
can feel "we know how to pray." Never. Nobody knows how
to pray, because it is God's business. It can be a great comfort to feel, "I went to mass this morning; I have prayed," or
"I spent a quiet time with the Bible this morning; I have
prayed." A devout Muslim could say, "I have faced Mecca
at the appointed times and said the ordained prayers; I have
prayed — that's it."

No, it is never it; there is not an "it." Just as in life you
do not do a spell of breathing in the morning and that is it;
you are breathing all the time, and if you stop breathing,
then you stop, you are dead. In a true sense, if you stop praying, you are dead. But this is a mystery known only to God.

When I started *The Story of Painting* in the caves at Las-
caux, I said that making art is one of the things that defines
us as human. I think the need to pray is an even more
profound characteristic. I said this once and my friends
laughed. They enlarged upon the viciousness of criminals,
the mindlessness of thugs and the banality of the money
obsessed. But at night, alone, unhappy, I cannot believe
there is anybody who does not feel a surge of anxious longing. Some poor brutal creature who has never heard of
God, perhaps never known human kindness, may still have
a yearning in his heart for something he cannot describe.

God, who knows exactly what we are, each of us, individually, what our genes are, what our upbringing has been, what our opportunities are, this God may well see this wordless, inchoate unhappiness as a form of prayer.

"God"

It seems to me that the most important thing in life is that all I am should be Jesus oriented. I say Jesus, because I am wary of using the word "God." Essentially, this is a meaningless word. No thoughts can encompass God. There is no box into which you can put Him. He, or for that matter, She, completely transcends any human concepts. When we say "God," we are doing no more than pointing a finger. It is a directional word. Forced to give a definition, all I could say is that God is Reality so absolute that all other realities are relative.

But none of this holds for Jesus. With Him we are on our own ground Here is one who is as human as we are, whose words are written down for us in the Scriptures. Jesus was the sole man who could look on God and know Him. "I and the Father are one" (John 10:30) and, again, "No one knows the Father but the Son and those to whom the Son chooses to reveal Him" (Matthew 11:27). Jesus chose to reveal the Father to anyone who would listen, and his revelation, something only He could know, was that God was Father. Knowing the Fatherhood of God is transformative, and it is only in Jesus that this knowledge comes.

I cannot imagine living without this awareness of God as Father, clinging to the spirit of Jesus, praying to have the mind of Jesus ("Have this mind amongst yourselves, which is yours in Christ Jesus," Philippians 2:5), for Him to love the world in me. But I am speaking from within Christianity, and I am quite certain that those who have another religion can become very close to God in their own way. They too must deal with the complete transcendence of God, but deal with it they do. Anyone who has had the privilege of seeing the solemn silent works of Buddhist or Hindu art can never doubt that here we have visual worship. In fact, since much of this art depicts the immense peace of God, they can be less disturbing to prayer than much Christian art.

I find it very painful to see paintings and sculptures that hold out before us the pain and suffering of Jesus. Here is someone I love depicted in agony. This is almost certainly a personal weakness. But I always have to step back emotionally and shield myself from the full impact of a picture of the Passion, whereas I can meet full on a Buddhist work of art or the wonderful arabesques of Muslim calligraphy. Notice I am speaking of art here and how the art of other religions shows us the reality of their prayer. They are not praying in Jesus, because Him they do not know. They are praying in the spirit of their own religion, making use of their own scaffolding of faith. But who else can they pray to except God, the one God? There is no other God but God. As a Christian I have no difficulty with this.

Scripture and the Eucharist

Caravaggio, that great dramatist, has seized upon one of the most dramatic incidents in the New Testament (figure 8). The risen Jesus has walked from Jerusalem to Emmaus with two of His grieving disciples. He has explained to them the Scriptures and why their Lord had to die. But although we hear that "their hearts burned within them" (Luke 24:32), at no moment did they recognize that their companion was Jesus Himself. They press Him to have a meal with them in the village, and then — and this is the moment that Caravaggio seizes upon — Jesus took bread, blessed and broke it, and "he was known to them in the breaking of the bread" (Luke 24:35).

This is an extraordinary witness to our need of the Eucharist. Caravaggio emphasizes it by showing other food, like the wonderful still life of fruit teetering on the edge of the table, as inadequate. It is Jesus Himself who is our food, our prayer. What always strikes me is that the words of Scripture that Jesus Himself had explained to these men did not reveal Him until there was this eucharistic action. If we are to pray with any seriousness, we must read Scripture. It is the Word of God. But if we are to recognize Jesus in Scripture, we need His grace. The two complement each other.

Holy Communion energizes everything we do. In its power we are taken into the sacrifice of Jesus, we are able to be broken bread for others to eat, but for that power to be fully active, we must bring to it a mind that has applied itself to understanding what is said in the Bible. Jesus is the Word of God who must animate and make real the written Word of God. Caravaggio's Jesus is a very unusual depiction: young, fresh, beardless. I think this jolts us out of our own conventions into the profundity of what is here set before us. Both disciples have clearly not broken their own bread. Jesus has given it to them. Caravaggio highlights it, as he does the pathetic legs of the dead chicken. If we enter into Holy Communion with an understanding of holy Scriptures, we will accept having the bread of self blessed, broken and given.

Why Aren't Christians Better People?

This is, sadly, a good question. Let me answer as a Catholic Christian, well aware that there are other churches in which God takes great delight. (When Evelyn Waugh was boasting about being a Catholic, someone who was smarting from his malice pointed out that he was no great advertisement for his faith. "Ah," said Waugh, "you must think how much worse I'd be if I wasn't a Catholic.") Why though? Why is our faith not more transformative?

The answer, of course, is that God's gifts do not work automatically. They will make us holy if we seriously commit ourselves to the truth of what is happening. Here we come to something tragic, the inadequacy of the teaching of the faith that leaves so many people unprepared to respond to the gifts of God. To regard the sacrament as an obligation, a chore, and a boring one at that, to be done on a Sunday, is a hideous travesty of the truth. Mass may indeed be boring, and the dear priest's sermon an affliction to be patiently endured (or, of course, an intellectual treat to be discussed throughout the week), but we do not go to mass for entertainment. A comparison could be made with parenting. If you feed and clothe and educate your child, you have done your duty. But what fatherhood and mother-hood is about is to be, to the child, all that a loving parent could be, for the child to be your joy. To be taken to the self-offering of Jesus to the Father is what being a Catholic is about, it is what the mass is about. How many understand this? And if it is not understood, whose fault is it? Some-where the meaning of the faith has been lost.

Of course, I am speaking here as a Catholic Christian. I would speak in the same manner if I were a Methodist, or a Baptist, or an Anglican. Each of us is here to worship God for what He is and not for what we can get from our worship.

Truly to believe is a terrible glory, very hard for weak and slothful humanity. One of the reasons why we pray is so that we will want to pray more. Not want in the sense of feel an emotional desire, but in the sense of need. Not to pray, not to be a true Christian, is to declare a reluctance to live life to the full. It is a choice of a small, warm, selfish life. However seductive the comfort of it is, it is the choice of a fool. The great life that is possible in God has infinitely more to offer. It would be like Rembrandt refusing to paint because he could live on his wife's money. We can see what a diminishment that would be: here was a man created to be a great artist. Yet, in a way, we are all created to be great artists, artists of a life, the one sole life that is possible with God's grace for each of us uniquely. Only in prayer is it possible for God to draw us out of the restrictions that we have unconsciously chosen.

We Know That the World Is Not Right

No one can prove that God exists. If we could prove it, why would we need faith? Faith is believing in what cannot be proved, but which we choose to accept.

This is not a blind and irrational choice. For those who are genuinely in doubt, I would point to the fact that we all know from within that our life does not satisfy us. The smallest child is enraged by injustice, and yet injustice is the norm. Pain, sorrow, death — these things wound us to the heart. We feel passionately that they are not right, and this is not how life should be.

Yet from where do we get that conviction? Pain, sorrow and death are the pattern of every life. It is that instinctive anger with the inadequacies of the life that we know that seems to me a pointer to the existence of God. Actual life on earth is short. But would a short, brutal life not satisfy us, with all its deficiencies, if we had no sense that this was not all we were born for? Faith tells us that the reality for

FIGURE 3. ORAZIO
GENTILESCHI—
The Lute Player, c. 1612–1620.
Image © 2006 Board of Trustees,
National Gallery
of Art, Washington.

FIGURE 4. PIERO DELLA
FRANCESCA—*The Baptism
of Christ.* © National
Gallery, London.

FIGURE 5. MARC CHAGALL—
The Sacrifice of Isaac, 1960–1966.
© 2007 Artists Rights Society (ARS),
New York, ADAGP, Paris.

FIGURE 6. GIAMBATTISTA
TIEPOLO—*The Martyrdom of
Saint Agatha*, c. 1745–1750.
© Bildarchiv Preussischer
Kulturbesitz/Art Resource, NY.

FIGURE 7. EL GRECO—*Christ on the Cross*. The J. Paul Getty Museum, Los Angeles.

FIGURE 8. CARAVAGGIO—*The Supper at Emmaus*, 1571–1610.
© National Gallery, London.

FIGURE 9. *Icon
of Mother and Child.*
Courtesy of the Temple
Gallery, London.

FIGURE 10. ALBERT HERBERT—*The Mountain*, 1991.
Private Collection, England & Co. Gallery, London,
The Bridgeman Art Library.

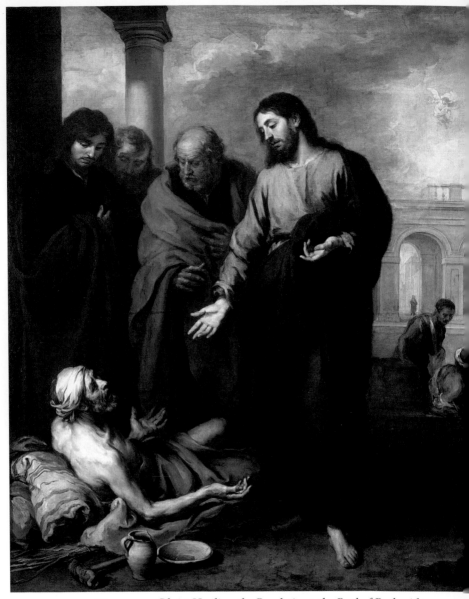

FIGURE 11. MURILLO—*Christ Healing the Paralytic at the Pool of Bethsaida.*
© The National Gallery, London.

FIGURE 12. JULES OLITSKI—*Judith Juice*, 1965.
© Estate of Jules Olitski / Licensed by VAGA,
New York, NY.

FIGURE 13. GRANT WOOD—*Spring Turning*, 1936. © Estate of Grant Wood / Licensed by VAGA, New York, NY.

which we were born is heaven, endless, eternal, as compared to the very brief spell of our life in time. It seems to me our hankering for more, our conviction that we are entitled to more, does at least suggest that there actually *is* more. I would never pretend to be a philosopher, or even that nobler creature, a theologian, but even just being alive and considering what our life is makes it at least possible that what religion says is true.

Admirable Atheists

Sometimes I blush for those who think themselves Christian, and yet the God they worship is cruel, suspicious, punitive and watchful. Who could love such a God? If that is your idea of God, you are obliged by all the rules of morality and common sense to become an atheist.

I have the greatest admiration for atheists, because by definition they have rejected a false "God." The true God, if you have the privilege of knowing Him, you cannot reject. Anybody who truly understands what God is cannot but believe and love. There are no lapsed Catholics, no lapsed Christians, but there are very many, far too many, who thought they were Catholics, or Christians, but did not have the good fortune to be taught the truth about God. They looked at this hideous image and said that if it was true, they refused to believe. Too few move on to the next stage and wonder if, in fact, their image of God is not true, or to the stage beyond when they realize that, in actuality, it is not true. If they could accept that the picture they have of God is wrong from the start, it would bring them to search for the truth.

Choice Not Feelings

You yourself have to choose God and search for Him. But you cannot choose God unless you have some understanding of what He is. If you have a false understanding, believing God to be a vicious tyrant, then woe betide you if you choose Him. That is not choosing God, but the nasty construct of debased human minds.

The real God is the one you see in the Gospels, and it is Jesus who gives that mysterious word "God" its meaning. In Jesus we can make this leap of faith believing that, despite all that happens, God is truly our Father.

It is you yourself who must choose God and search for Him. In other words, pray. This is what maturity means. You have no means of knowing how many other people have committed themselves to this lonely and rather frightening search. It seems to me that nobody can really help you with it or tell you how to do it. Only you as a responsible human being can make this turning of mind and heart away from self in the small sense and out to God. You have to accept that you may get no comeback from this, comforting you with a sense of rightness. Some people get a great deal of emotional support from their prayer. Others get nothing. Either way, comforting prayer or stark prayer is equally real, equally blessed.

I cannot tell you how passionately I would like to help people realize that what we feel does not essentially matter. This is especially true of prayer. I write this with a sinking feeling that most of you will not believe me. It is so natural for us to accept that what we feel is an image of objective reality. But it is not. Feelings come and go. They have no solidity to them. You can build nothing lasting on feeling. Think of happiness: what is it? It is not a feeling. It is something lasting for me, that is based upon the love of God. Any relationship, whether with God or man, that has only feeling to support it is in trouble. When the feeling goes (and it will), what have you left? Nothing. Whereas if you have made a rational choice and cling to it, what you have endures.

Art and Prayer

What has art to do with prayer? Speaking absolutely, nothing. Prayer has to do with God, ever present, ever loving, and with you yourself, as present and receptive of His love as you are able. Nothing else at all, the state of your health, your state of mind, even your state of goodness, is important. (What is missing, God will make clear to you — and if you truly desire Him, you will listen.) But if we come to speaking less absolutely and more relatively, then what you offer God in prayer is dependent on many factors. He can come only to the real you, and that totally true person, who has become what God intends him or her to become, is not what we are born with. We are born with the potential. It takes a long time of resolute desire to bring all the elements of this potential into active existence. And it is here that art matters.

Jesus told us that He had come so that we might have life and live it to the full. That "full" includes responding to the wonders of our world, experiencing them so as to be wholly alive. Friendship, the natural world, music, books, film — the list is very long. High on it, it seems to me, comes art.

I have always been saddened to find how many people think that the enjoyment of art is an elite pursuit, one for which they are either not educated or not intelligent enough. Of course this is nonsense. We are all born with the capacity to respond to art. Even our remote ancestors in their dark caves created works so beautiful that they have never been surpassed: equaled, yes; surpassed, never. I was lucky in coming early to an understanding of the spiritual depth that visual pleasure (and perturbation too — art elicits many layered responses) could provide. Although I am as yet far from being the Sister Wendy I was born to be, I acknowledge with gratitude that I am much closer, more integrated, more alive because of my contemplation of art. So in this sense, that of drawing one into a more profound awareness of one's own unique humanity, yes, art does matter to prayer. I have only to see a Cézanne, for example, perhaps one of his great landscapes, or a majestic still life, a landscape in its own right, and I am overwhelmed with joy. This is a profound and transforming joy, a call to enter into something beyond what is seen, something that Cézanne (or Poussin, or whoever) also saw but expressed in terms of light and color. There are no words for this, but I know that I have been lifted out of my smallness into something immeasurably great, something that, however vaguely, seems "holy."

It was to share the wonder of this experience that I have spent what would have been good silence time in writing and talking on the screen. Whatever people believed or did not believe, and I had no way of determining who would read or listen to me, this pure clarifying joy, with its implicit challenge, its awareness of what is beautiful, would be accessible. I carefully avoided any words that demanded faith, or faith in one religion rather than another. Since most world art is, in fact, religious, this has never been completely possible.

Yet, speaking now personally and without an agenda, I have come across works where I am moved, not only by the beauty of what I see, that beauty that is God, whether the theme be Botticelli's *Venus* or Degas' *Jockeys* or Fra Angelico's *Heaven*, but by something more particular. I have been touched by a religious insight, a "message," if you like, that I would not elaborate on in public, and yet which for me held great significance. These works that deeply affect me — me as a praying woman — are rare, but I treasure them. In that they directly unite me to God, I could say that they have a relevance to my prayer. I would never want to use them during prayer, but when I come to pray, what they have shown me may be a powerful incentive to surrender.

Icon of Mother and Child

The image that is most significant to me I have in card form, always here on my narrow — too narrow — all-purpose table. It is an icon of the Virgin and Child, probably painted about 550, say the scholars, and it is a very recent discovery (figure 9). The iconoclasts, who thought all images led to idolatry, ravaged their way through the Eastern Empire in the late seventh and eighth centuries. Only seven icons before this period have survived, five in Rome, which was never violated by the iconoclasts, and two in the far-away monastery of Saint Catherine in Sinai. Now the Temple Gallery in London has found an eighth, and I can never tire of gazing at it.

This icon may have come from some small church in Egypt, and miraculously survived, dirty and creased, from that age of faith into the age of disbelief. The Virgin does not engage us with her attention, nor does she look at her small Son. She removes herself from the scene, abstracting herself so that we might look only at Jesus. She is remarkably beautiful, with her pale, oval face and columnar neck, noble head held high as she turns away to the right and holds out to us the transparent mandala in which her Son sits. At first I thought this was her womb, but we can see her hand holding firmly to an edge. (Scholars, who of course are fascinated by this survival, think there may be a reference to the shield on which the face of Caesar was displayed to the army.)

Mary does right to diminish her presence — all she has ever wanted was for us to see Jesus. But this Jesus is unlike any representation of Christ that I have ever seen. He is neither baby nor adult, but small, intensely dignified, a majestic little figure with unruly auburn curls and large dark eyes. What makes Him so unique is His expression. All images of Christ, excepting those that show Him as a little baby, see Him as in control. Even Christ in His Passion is at peace, one who knows the answer. But here the small face is not at peace. This is an anxious child, and He fixes those questioning eyes on us not to tell us what His Father wants, but to invite us to search with Him. It has never bothered me to imagine what Jesus looked like. The Gospel writers were wholly unconcerned with how He appeared. Their only concern was what He meant, who He was. But if we had lived in first-century Palestine and met Jesus there, I cannot but feel that this deep probing look, drawing us into a spiritual journey that we are to take with Him, might have been more true to what we would have seen. I look at this face with a shock of wonder: it draws us away — but to where? Into mystery, into faith, into that Truth that Jesus has said He actually was, in His person: "I am the way, the truth, and the life" (John 14:6). The weight of that awareness rests almost visibly upon this small face. Does Jesus Himself understand it? We are taken into the mystery.

When this icon was in the Temple Gallery, Dick Temple kept a lamp burning before it, and with the electric lights dimmed the effect was indescribable. Several who saw it there were impelled to their knees — it imposes that quiet in which prayer is at home. Remember that this is specifically an icon, which means it was not painted as "art" but as a means to union with God. The unknown painter, all those centuries ago, would have fasted and kept vigil, would have prayed in silence and with words of supplication, begging to be made a vehicle in which God could come closer to us. The art world is rather baffled by icons, which fit into no histories of the development of painting and have only one purpose: to take us through what is seen to the Holy that is unseen. To ask an icon painter what art and prayer have to do with each other would be meaningless because here art is prayer. But only here.

Doubts

A priest once wrote to me referring to Saint Thomas, who doubted (as the Gospels tell us) and said that unless he put his finger into the wound in the side of Jesus, he would not believe in the Resurrection. My friend said he thought doubt was fruitful. It seems to me, rather, that doubt is irrelevant. Common enough, but not crucial to our relationship with God. It is what we do with the doubt that matters.

The holiest person I know has never had the slightest interior intimation that God exists. All she gets back from her prayer is doubt and darkness. She experiences a terrible fear that her life with God is all imagination, that there is no God, that living as a nun is a mockery. With this agonizing sense of her own personal weakness and her own absolute absence of felt certainty, she chooses. She chooses to believe. She chooses to act in accordance with that belief, which means in practice a life of heroic charity. This woman — and others like her, because she is not alone in this heroism — is giving to God the real sacrifice of faith. This woman chooses to love God and to serve Him and to believe in Him, even if she gets nothing back. It is a glory to know that she exists and that there are others like her.

No Reward for Prayer

Biblical themes have impressed themselves so deeply into Albert Herbert's imagination that he comes back to them again and again, always with new insights. Moses making his lonely journey up the mountain where the mystery of God awaits him is one such theme (figure 10). In this painting the mountain surges almost off the top of the canvas, pointing away into infinity, while Moses stands exposed, arms wide open to receive the divine message.

Perhaps he also opens his arms as a means of balance. He is terrifyingly high, planted as solidly as he can manage, with feet set apart and body tense with desire. He has reached this height by ways we cannot fathom — the mountain is precipitous, right-angled in its rejection of the easy ascent, and we realize that Moses has clambered to the meeting place with immense difficulty. No wonder he is stripped to his shirt, and his face is dark with fatigue. Not only does he present his own plea, but he represents the whole of creation: those who stand at the mountain foot, holding hands, afraid of the lonely responsibility of ascent, afraid too, perhaps, of having to risk life and limb on a climb into apparent nothingness.

But Moses also takes within his spirit the animal and vegetable world, the little living beasts that creep on the lower slopes and the great lovely tree that adorns them.

It is a beautiful mountain, alive with so much color and fascination, yet Moses has to labor on through it all, leaving everything behind, if he is to be present before his God.

He has not, we feel sure, turned away in any sense of belittlement. Herbert takes such loving artistic pains to show us the sweetness of the innocent and material world that we cannot but feel that Moses, too, related tenderly to it. But nothing can go up with him except his bare self. Humbly, he does not press on to the uppermost peak, but stops on a convenient plateau, where God can address him and he can listen. It is easy to see why this scene exerts such force over Herbert; it is the quintessential image of prayer.

Mystic after mystic has written of this solitary ascent and the need to labor along the way, the need to strip the heart of all that is a distraction, the need to hold on in faith to the certainty that God is there, even if—especially if—we see nothing.

"Nothing, nothing, nothing on the way," said Saint John of the Cross, "and on the mountain, nothing." Nothing but God alone.

THREE

Prayer and Personality

The Fullness of Life

Writing to a fellow poet, Robert Duncan (1927–89) says the Chinese philosopher Confucius asserts that there are three supreme virtues in living. All of them, it seems to me, have an immediate relevance to prayer.

The first is what Duncan calls "the effort," which must be his translation of *Qi*, the divine energy that infuses all that is. In Eastern art, landscape has a significance far beyond anything in the art of the West. For the Chinese, a mountain is a spiritual statement, not a material fact, and so is a stream or a cloud or a tree. Scholars kept rocks on their desks or in their courtyards, because in their very materiality they reminded them of, and united them to, this sacred *Qi*: a radiant power greater than our own, holding in active tension the whole of nature, which includes human nature, in its great orbit. But whereas landscape and nature are inherently imbued with *Qi*, it is a grace that human beings must actively and seriously pursue. They have to enter into *Qi* consciously; it is not a given.

With a slight twist of emphasis, we might call *Qi* the Holy Spirit. The Holy Spirit is God made actual to us, God working within us, God lifting us to Himself in prayer. Whenever we speak about prayer, we are really speaking about the power of the Holy Spirit ("for we do not know how to pray as we ought, but the Spirit Himself intercedes for us with sighs too deep for words," Romans 8:26). We are not conscious of this all-powerful Spirit, nor can we be. He eludes all our perceptions. But we should acknowledge the truth of His presence. If we say prayer is God's business, this is essentially what we mean: that all that is alive and real in our prayer comes from His presence. Turn to God, and it is the Holy Spirit who has drawn you. Rest in Him, and it is the Holy Spirit who sustains you. Go forth in His Spirit to work for the truth, and all that is pure and good in what you do is not yours, but His.

Humility

The second of Confucius's "supreme virtues in living" is not to be great, but to be an unknown. There can never be any true prayer when, at some level, we regard this as an expression of our moral importance. Forget what others think or may think of us, humility, which is surely what is exercising the mind of Confucius, demands that we ourselves are uninterested in what we are. Humility is nothing to do with having a low opinion of our qualities; it is all to do with not being interested in them, not gazing long and devotedly at yourself.

What does it matter how clever, how skillful, how powerful you might be, and what does it matter that others recognize this or not? When Jesus spoke about being like little children, I am sure that He meant the willingness to accept the unimportance of a child in first-century Palestine. Whatever a child's insights, its very childishness would militate against anybody paying attention to it. Be content to be a nobody, says Jesus. Accept that you get no feedback from others as to how good you are, how pure your prayer. Live in the shadows, and let God have all the glory.

One of the real dangers of living a life of prayer is that you can start to examine your soul and dwell, either with contrition or with gratitude, upon qualities that you find within yourself. This self-centeredness comes well disguised as a desire for purity. But our center is God, is Jesus. Scraping away at yourself, peering inward — this is a narrowing of the freedom and the joy that is natural to prayer. Forget yourself. Let God purify you. Look at Him and be at peace.

Being Human

The third of the supreme virtues in living as explained by Confucius is the most unexpected. It is to be visited by friends from afar. I must admit the lyrical bathos of this took me aback (I, who never like any visitors, near or far). But one can see what he means.

The great danger of a commitment to prayer is not only thinking oneself special, as I have just described, but embarking on a certain isolation. Yet all of us are members of a community. All that God gives us in prayer is not just for ourselves, but for others. We come to Him, we pray to Him as one of a great family. This family, His human children, can never be superhuman. Joy and pleasure are part of living in His real world. Confucius regards visits from faraway friends as being a source of joy and comfort, something that our psyche actually needs. Cut out pleasure and the relaxations of love and laughter, and we are not more given to God, but less.

Sometimes there can be a fear that a life of prayer is a gray life, without friends, without humor, without parties, without pleasure. No, indeed, it is a life of multicolored beauty, not necessarily, or for most people, ever in the prayer itself, but in the awareness of life that comes from prayer. Being close to God means we are close to all He created. The devout can find this concept difficult. Think of Jesus and the Pharisees, who scorned him as a glutton and a wine-bibber because he so obviously enjoyed life. If our prayer narrows and hardens us, there is something wrong.

Prayer and Sin

Since prayer is essentially an attitude, a desire for God, the one thing that stops it dead is sin. It need not even be actual sin, a deliberate refusal to obey the will of God, but rather sinfulness, an abiding state of almost unconscious selfishness. Sinfulness, which coalesces and becomes evident in actual sin, makes mockery of a professed desire to pray. It closes the heart, turns the eyes inward toward oneself, rather than outward toward love.

Obviously, there is some element of sinfulness in all of us and a genuine desire to pray will expose the desire not to pray, which we would like to pretend does not exist. A holy Jesuit once said to me, speaking of himself, "There is part of me that wants no part of Him." Even to think of this makes one sad, and yet it must be true, or God would so take possession of us that we would be radiant with His light. If we are not, why are we not? It is the sloth and the egotism of sinfulness that block His power.

I think the distinction between sin and sinfulness is important. One sin, with God's help, we can escape: "Lead us not into temptation but deliver us from evil." When we pray, God does deliver us. Remember that to commit a sin is not an act of impulse, it is a deliberate refusal to do what our conscience clearly indicates is right. Goodness or badness, sin wills to be bad. I sometimes think this does not happen very often. If it does happen, there is the sacrament of reconciliation in which to express our sorrow and receive the total forgiveness and renewal of spirit that it is God's delight to offer. There seems little point in talking about prayer if we are in a state of refusal of God.

But prayer and sinfulness go hand in hand, because sinfulness is part of the human condition. Sinfulness is that weakness of will that we detest in ourselves but cannot jettison. We all desire from our hearts to be good, to be loving and humble and patient, strong, kind, firm. We also know that desire does not confer these qualities. We have to practice over the years and learn how to be good. God's grace comes infallibly through prayer. Want to be good, and you will become good, but at a cost. It is the cost that is the test of the sincerity of our prayer, of our desire.

Saint Francis de Sales, for example, became renowned for his patience, perhaps the distinctive mark of his holiness. But he was born violently impatient, and it took years of struggle and sacrifice, of wrestling with his instinctive irritation and anger, before he mellowed into his eventual gentleness. It was his union with God in prayer, his longing to be made different, that made it possible for God to transform him. God will do the work, but we must be there for it to be done, and prayer is, above all, that "being there."

Self-deception

One of the sad results of our sinfulness is that it blurs our capacity to see truth. This is surely what is meant by "original sin." Original sin is not a stain on the soul; it is not actually a sin at all, and it is, in fact, a misleading expression. Who could think that babies are sinful? No, babies are simply human. And to be born human is to be born weak and blinded — not wholly, of course, but sufficiently diminished from our true potential so as not to understand the way in which we evade our Lord. Think of Adam and Eve hiding away in the undergrowth from God, refusing to accept blame, prevaricating. Before the fall, they could look at God and walk with Him in the evening as His children, His friends; after the fall they entered into what I can only call a state of moral muddle. This is a poetic explanation of the state in which we find ourselves. Accepting the full extent of our selfishness and our lazy denial of responsibility is very difficult for us.

One of the reasons why I always feel it dangerous to write or talk about prayer is that it can be a psychological cloak for our lack of true commitment. It is so much easier to talk about things than to do them. It is so much more comforting to feel that one is spiritual (after all, do I not read books on prayer, am I not eager to discuss it?) than actually to follow the austere and painful life of the spirit. And conversely, our lack of "experience" can also be an excuse. I long to tell myself that the reason why I cannot pray is that I have never been taught, the right books have passed me by, the holy guru never came down my street. Hence the eager interest in books and articles on prayer — all obscuring from me my lack of true desire. Hence the enthusiasm for the holy retreat givers, the spiritual directors, who will serve me as irrefutable alibis. If there were more to do, would I not do it? (I fast twice a week, I give tithes of all I possess . . .) No, I would not do it; I have no intention of doing it, but of course, to admit this to myself would rack me with guilt.

Remember the rich young man in the Gospel? He had all the right words: "Good Master, what must I do?" And Jesus tried to jolt him into reality. Why use words like "good" when you do not understand them? But the young man persisted, and Jesus gave him what he truly believed he was asking for. Jesus tells him what to do, and of course he goes away sorrowful, because Jesus has taken it out of the region of ideals and emotions and rendered His Father's claims in plain fact: "Sell, give, come follow me." It was not what was wanted. Do you think this man went away conscious of his inner falsehood and realizing that he was quite unprepared to look at God straight? I hope he did, but I fear that he may well have been sad because the Master's claims "could not" be met, that he barricaded himself behind the excuse of "inability," which he convinced himself he longed to be able to overcome.

One of the effects of prayer is that it exposes us to ourselves. If we pray, that comfortable cloak that assures us of our virtue begins to fray, to dissipate, to uncover the sorry nakedness of what we really are. When people say they have difficulty in prayer, or they are getting nowhere, or that it just seems a waste of time, they are being drawn into this divine spotlight that makes us profoundly uncomfortable. It would be masochistic to want to know the extent of our sinfulness, but we cannot offer ourselves to God until we have accepted the painful truth of how little we really love Him. This is hateful. We can take courage if prayer reveals something positive that we can do, for example, if it shows us that we are being thoughtless at home, or unkind in the office, or greedy at the table. Then we can make resolutions and set to work, asking God for the grace to become the person He intends. But sometimes no actual lack of love becomes clear to us, just our sense of spiritual failure. However this humiliates or hurts, it is a precious grace. We can see how profoundly, infinitely, we need the purification that God offers us, and our willed desire to pray should be immensely reinforced. "All things work to the good of those who love Him," and plumbing the smelly depths of our sinfulness is a perfect example.

Helplessness

This image of *Christ Healing the Paralytic at the Pool of Bethsaida* has always seemed to me rich with spiritual symbolism (figure 11). Murillo, that devout artist, would have been well aware of this. The paralytic, remember, did not ask Jesus to heal him. The Gospels simply tell us that he lay there helpless. He had no one to carry him into the therapeutic waters of the pool. (The presence of the angel in the upper right corner shows that the time is right for a miraculous healing.) It is Jesus Himself who takes the initiative, who comes across to him and gives him back his health. What Murillo seems to understand so profoundly is this state of wordless entreaty, of human helplessness, of a need too great to be expressed. We can see that the man has squatter's rights to that corner of the pool: there are his plate and his jug, his sleeping bag. Without any explicit hope, he simply offers himself in all his poverty to Jesus.

This expresses visually our state when we pray. Of course, there is always space for an explicit intention, should we be so moved. Others who were healed by Jesus came to Him and asked. But how much deeper is this state of poverty, of surrender, of abandonment to whatever it pleases God to do or to give? All prayer in a way acts out the intercourse between Jesus and the cripple, between the Son of God and the beggar. Holding out those empty hands is what draws the healing gesture of the Savior's hand. Those who feel able to go themselves into the healing waters of the pool, or those who have friends to take them, do not attract the compassionate heart of Jesus. I sometimes think that those who feel they can do it on their own or can be helped represent all the people who want to pray, but will not accept that it is God's business and that nobody else can show us how to do it. The how is in the helplessness and also in the courage to stay there, looking at Jesus, accepting the loneliness of responsibility. No one can heal this man; only God. His part is to surrender himself.

Guilt

When we pray, we must try to come to God in peace. One of the great disrupters of peace is the corroding effect of a sense of guilt. We must not confuse guilt with contrition. Contrition is healing. It is a trustful sorrow for our sins that looks at God and knows that He will heal us. But guilt does not look at God. It looks at ourselves and our misdoings. It does not trust God and will not let Him heal us.

Guilt and remorse go round and round on a treadmill of regret, whereas prayer sets us free from any treadmill and takes us into the peace of being loved. There is something very selfish about guilt, clinging like a naughty baby to the rattle of our own self-importance. Whatever we have done, God forgives it and forgets it. His sorrow is that, in sinning, we have damaged ourselves, not Him. Every real sin narrows our capacity to receive Him. Any real act of contrition offers us to God for Him to restore us.

I am not talking about emotion. Some temperaments are deeply drawn to the feeling of guilt. This feeling has to be suffered and repudiated. If we are given to remorse, unfortunate us, we cannot will it away and want to feel different; we have to accept that the feeling is false and damaging and refuse to wallow in it. If it means turning to God a hundred times a minute to be liberated from our selfish human guilt, then a hundred times a minute we turn to Him. This may not be very comfortable prayer, but it is true prayer. We are acknowledging that the holy name Jesus means "Savior."

Reconciliation

Speaking as a Catholic Christian, I feel strongly, though I am willing to accept I may be mistaken, that the great sacrament of reconciliation — what used to be called "confession" — is not for trivialities. If we have snubbed an office junior, snapped at our children, made up an excuse to avoid helping a friend, we have only to turn to God and express our "sorry," and all is forgiven. Where the sacrament of reconciliation comes into its full strength is either in confessing something tremendous ("I destroyed a marriage"), which, of course, God has already forgiven if we are sorry, but which psychologically we ourselves may need to make formal confession of, or in bringing to the sacrament our sinfulness: we do not love Him enough. Confessing this offers our Lord the opportunity to lift us up into His own love for the Father, and the sacrament leaves us energized with the energy of Jesus. It is a mystery to me why it is not appreciated.

There is an extraordinary ignorance about this sacrament. Some people even seem unaware that absolution is dependent on a firm purpose of amendment. The sacrament is meant to change the way the penitent is living, and if there is no determination to change, the sacrament cannot be received. Why go, though, if there is no desire to come closer to the heart of God? And why not go if there is such a desire? Some people find it very much more difficult than others, but there again, feelings are to be ignored. For those in the Catholic tradition, the sacrament of reconciliation is one of the great means by which one is united to God in prayer. It purifies us, by taking us into the purity of our Lord. There could be no better preparation for prayer.

We must always remember too that it is not just a question of telling my Father that I am sorry: it is *our* Father. My sin or my sinfulness (or lack of love) affects all my brothers and sisters. The spiritual atmosphere of the world changes when anybody damages their capacity to receive God's love. So in confessing to a priest — making it formal, as it were — I make formal acknowledgment of this responsibility to everybody. With all our other personal relationships we need only to say "sorry" to the person we have hurt. But our relationship with the world is so all-embracing that purely personal contrition is not enough. It is enough for forgiveness, and if God and I were the only ones who mattered, we could leave it at that. But as we all know, even if perhaps only in theory, no man is an island. And what we do, however little we can see it, has effects that are global. I admit this sounds a little over the top, but the spiritual climate that makes it harder or easier to be good is the creation of the whole world. And to that world, however reluctantly, I belong. And so do you.

Forgiveness

When Jesus answered the apostles' plea by giving them the Lord's Prayer, he did not emphasize that we should love one another, but rather that we should forgive one another. I sometimes feel that many of us suffer from hidden anger, painful memories of slights, and worse, persecutions, that we can will to forgive. It seems to be a cultural trend today that there is always somebody to blame. If we are completely at a loss, there are always genetics and our parents! It may well be true that each of us is wounded, but dwelling on the wounds and the scars and the hurt and the mutilations takes us straight back to self and away from God. What has happened to you, and whose fault it is, is not really your affair. It is for you to ask God for the grace of a blanket forgiveness, forgiving without even knowing in what way you were damaged. If we cannot drop the desire to be justified, we are shutting ourselves off from God.

Remember always this is not a matter of how you feel. Emotionally, you may be scarred forever by some betrayal; you may be unable to forget it. With all your heart, though, you cling to God and pray to forgive it. Let me repeat: it is the will to forgive that matters. After all, God alone knows how deliberate or "evil," this betrayal was: have we not quite innocently in our own time damaged other people?

The whole roiling mass of our pains and suspicions are antipathetic to the surrender to God that we desire in prayer. We choose Him, we choose to forgive as our Father in heaven forgives, and we trust Him to transform us into men and women who truly love. About the feelings of hurt or betrayal we can do nothing. Or rather, we can offer them actively and consciously to God. The more we pray, the more we become aware of our own need for forgiveness. Yet God, freely offering His forgiveness, is all too aware that we cannot accept its blessing if we still harbor rancor against others in our hearts. In a sense, one of the reasons why we offer ourselves in prayer is to be forgiven, brought nearer the holiness of God and enabled by His grace to draw others into forgiveness.

Deadly Sins

The theologians of the Middle Ages loved making lists and arranging things numerically. They decided there were seven deadly sins: pride, envy, anger, gluttony, sloth, lust and covetousness. This is not the list, if we were given to making lists, that we might draw up today. Gluttony, for example, seems to have meant something rather different in the Middle Ages. Probably most people will overeat if given a chance, but that hardly qualifies as a deadly sin. True gluttony, I am told, involves stuffing yourself to vomiting point again and again and again. This is surely extraordinarily rare. Anger, too, or wrath, can be soul destructive, as in road rage at its worst, but even road rage is not at this deadly pitch of sin. Envy and covetousness are unpleasant traits we understand and must guard against, but they are surely not "deadly." Even lust, which to so many people seems to be the sin par excellence, the one thing that is truly wrong, could be better understood perhaps if seen not in itself, but as a form of the one sin that is truly deadly, which is pride.

Pride has nothing to do with conceit or being a snob. Nor is it that rightful and laudable sense of pleasure that we all feel over some personal triumph, however minor. The young cook bringing from the oven her first soufflé should be flushed with pride, good pride, happy pride.

Sinful pride is something dark and repulsive, and it lies behind all human cruelties. How can there be ethnic cleansing if there is not contempt? How can one race of people massacre their neighbors if they regard them as creatures with equal rights? The horrors of racism, of religious intolerance, all stem from pride, an overvaluation of what we are and a contempt for the different one. Pride is the perverted conviction that only *I* matter. Other people are for my use, whether I use their bodies (lust) or their goods (covetousness). They have no rights; I alone have rights.

We are told that rape is far less connected with sex than it is with power, and the desire for power, of course, is the outward expression of pride. Using and abusing, fettered by no appreciation or sympathy or respect for others, is the essence of this evil. It ranges all the way from cruelty, when we take pleasure in the suffering of other people or even of animals, through the various degrees of selfishness. When the serpent in the garden allured Adam and Eve with the promise that eating the forbidden fruit would make them as gods, this is what was meant. The sad irony is that this god-attitude of the proud shuts the sinner away from the reality of God into the stifling narrowness of being one's own god. There is an element of this in all of us, and it is in prayer that we begin to realize how hideously self-centered we are at heart. How little we want to recognize the rights of others when they clash with ours. If we are honest, have we not all found that the needs of others can be an irritation? One man's tragedy is another man's annoyance. The feeling of annoyance is not sinful. It is only if we give physical expression to annoyance or impatience that we fail. But acknowledging the presence of these negative feelings alerts us to our need to be more loving.

All the deadly sins seem to fit under the shade of pride except for sloth. This has its own nasty place. Sloth is the zombie sin, the refusal to accept responsibility for what we are. To be human means to have duties. Sloth shrugs them away, slides them onto other shoulders, will not bear the burden of being human.

Both these sins can coexist with a good deal of apparent piety. It was said of the nuns of Port-Royal that they were as pure as angels and as proud as devils. And as for sloth, we have all known people whose apparent gentleness and detachment is little more than a tranquil laziness.

If there were no other purpose in praying than to have our tendencies revealed to us, prayer would still be the instinctive choice of those who call themselves Christians. Only God knows how proud and how selfish we are, and He longs to purify us with the fire of His presence.

Virtue

If pride regards other people as fodder for its own desires and ambitions, and sloth is concerned with nobody but itself, the opposite is obviously the one great fundamental virtue, which is love.

"Love," though, is an ambivalent word. We use it very freely, from meaning delight in, as in "I love Mozart" (or spinach, or traveling in Hungary), through to the most common use, which is that of romantic passion, as in the tenderness of Romeo and Juliet or the steamy embraces of Antony and Cleopatra. So the most profound meaning, love of God, can sometimes be colored and attenuated by these other meanings lurking in our subconscious (I once wrote a book called *The Mystery of Love,* and a journalist said to me in surprise, "What a raunchy title!"). The word I prefer to use is "reverence." "Respect," if you like, though I think that "reverence" is more all-embracing.

"Reverence" means complete acceptance of other people and even of other things, letting them have their own place and their own weight. Where pride seeks to manipulate, reverence seeks to set free. It wants only the good of the other. If we love, we will never take advantage. God treats us with this reverence, allowing us to be, even when in our laziness and fear we would like Him to take over. He will stand with us, supporting us to become all that is possible, but out of love God will never constrain. Reverence keeps us from the seductive pitfall of believing that the end justifies the means. It never does. If we truly respect the means, we will not even attempt to subordinate it to the great good of the end. The means is its own end.

It is simple to talk about love or reverence, but this virtue is extremely difficult to practice. This is not so much because it is costly, though it can be, but because it is hard to know what exactly love or reverence demands. Every parent knows that always saying yes to your children is not the most loving way to treat them. But when does one say yes and when does one say no? The outward action is no guarantee of inward love. Saint Paul speaks about giving all one's property to the poor and even one's body to be burned—becoming a martyr—and adds that if these heroic deeds "are without love," they are spiritually useless. It is not just what we do, but why we do it, and sometimes how we do it. We encounter these subtleties every day, deciding, making choices, trying to do what is right.

I have come to the conclusion that whatever our goodwill, love depends upon wisdom. A false reverence may be an escape from decision, in other words laziness, or even an expression of a desire to seem reverent: pride. But in prayer we are illuminated by the wisdom of God. Jesus told us He would send us the Holy Spirit, the Spirit of wisdom. We will not be told explicitly by some divine voice what it is best to do. God in His courtesy would not presume. But we will be inwardly enlightened so that we can "read" the circumstances that confront us and respond to them with what, to quote Saint Paul again, is the "mind of Christ." Without that mind of Christ, that holy and unselfish wisdom that puts others first and wants only their good, there is no love, there is no reverence. It is ours for the asking.

Passion

In some ways abstract art has a natural affinity with prayer. In fact, the first great exhibition of abstract art was titled *The Art of the Spiritual.* Like prayer, an abstract picture is not "about" anything. There are no shapes that relate to material objects. It is what it is. And if the artist gives his picture a name as here — *Judith Juice* — in no sense is he trying to summon the image of an individual or even to recall in an abstract way a facet of his or her personality (figure 12).

Olitski has created an intense fusion of color, form and texture. Every element not only has space to breathe but is present in the picture because it draws into more intense life every other element. Not only is there coexistence, but there is that unforced mutual acceptance that makes each color more itself, more totally focused because of the complementary hue beside it. That startling blue is deepened by the shimmering white along the central borders and it, in turn, draws from the intense orange on three sides all its capacity for "orangeness." The orange makes the dark blue more totally itself. The result is an intense radiance as we are drawn into the depths of that concentrated central oblong.

But this intensity, this passion, is not wild or uncontrolled. It is achieved through the trained intellect and learned skill of the artist. Passion is not wild emotion; it can be deliberate choice. The passion for God that arises from prayer — and which can arise only there, where God takes possession and loves within us — is never a narrowing passion. It does not drive out our other desires, but integrates them and gives them meaning. Because God is all that matters, everything else at last begins to matter as it should. Love becomes universal, not only allowing others their own truth-to-self, but actively helping them to attain it, as the blue and orange do to each other in the painting. Freedom, warmth, a security so vast that it can take all risks and not see them as frightening: all this is the result of an absolute directedness to God and God alone.

But it is a passion of directedness that exists in being, not in feeling. *Judith Juice* is not a proclamation, it is an actuality, a painting that one man brought slowly and surely into existence. It is our actions, the life we lead, that make actual the intensity that God silently infuses when we are at prayer. These works, the making real of our prayer in our daily life, are not the result of our own energies. They come not from us, but from Him, just as the work of art is from the artist's paint and energies. Our part is to want to want to surrender our potential to His Will.

Faith

Like love, "faith" is a word that seems simple but is, in fact, complex. I have heard people praising "simple faith." What they are referring to is an almost rote reception of mass and the sacraments based on pitifully slight knowledge of the teaching of our Blessed Lord. What they are really describing is ignorant faith, lazy faith, a refusal to engage the revelation of God with the full dimensions of what we are or what we can be. Faith is not meant to be a comfort blanket, as those of "simple faith" tend to make it. It is a strenuous call to engage all we are with the Father of Jesus.

We must bring our minds to our faith, not just our hearts. Faith does not mean ticking off our assent to dogma, although that may pass for faith. True faith, the virtue of faith, entails a profound involvement with the truth of Jesus. We have to understand it. Unless we know what "the Gospel" really is and the fullness of what Jesus had to tell us, our faith can be a surface thing. We can say, and it is a boast that Saint Teresa of Avila made proudly, that we are children of the Church. What the Church teaches, that we believe. True enough, but the Church grows and develops.

In the nineteenth century the Church, speaking through Pope Pius IX, issued an absolute condemnation of socialism, freedom of the press and freedom of conscience.

In the climate of the times this may have been a necessary prophylactic against corrosive and seductive doubt. We now see it as absurdly restrictive of the human capacity to understand. The pope was also rabidly opposed to any division between Church and State, something we now take for granted. If we accept that the Church is made of human beings who live at a specific time and must share the culture of that time, we can understand that it is a living organism that not only will, but must, change. Our duty is to obey the Church and to make use of the unique access to God that our faith offers. It is never imperative to think that the last word has been spoken on any doctrine.

In our own times the obvious area where the Church will develop is in that of sexuality. Some would say there is still a medieval mind-set at the Vatican with regard to this profoundly disturbing element of our nature, in that some strictures of the Old Testament are still taken literally, whereas others — like the profaning proximity of a menstruating woman — are not. There is so little love in the world; why then should homosexual love be suspect? If there is fidelity and true commitment, what distinguishes this kind of love from another? But whatever we may think and believe to be true, we are called by our faith to obey. If we think that Church teaching has got it wrong in any way, we have only to wait. It is God's Church. The Spirit of Jesus will always be with it to "the very end of time."

This is just one example of our need to delve deeply into the teachings of faith. I have been horrified to find people who call themselves Catholics having so poor an understanding of what the Church actually teaches. Christology, that most beautiful branch of theology, has pondered deeply upon the mystery of Jesus. We today are in a position, if we take the trouble, to understand the Gospels as never before. If we pray, we are almost impelled toward the Scriptures, the New Testament above all. We need constantly to read the Gospels and epistles and think about them. (By definition faith means there is no proof. There are arguments that suggest the truth, but if we could lay it down in a scientific formula, there would be no need of faith.) Anyone who says they wish they could believe but they have not been given the gift of faith misunderstands the nature of faith. It is indeed a gift, and God holds it out to everyone. Whether or not you feel it is true is irrelevant. Oh, how one needs to stress and repeat that feelings are merely subjective. If you want faith, ask for it. God gladly gives it. Then, with this newborn faith, you can begin the long and lovely process of understanding what it is to which you have committed yourself. You read, you pray, you say with the desperate man in the Gospel, "I believe; help my unbelief" (Mark 9:24).

Love always seeks knowledge. And the more we want to love God, the more we will want to understand who it is we love. The more we understand, the deeper our faith, the more absolute our love. Love is the consequence of faith, and we can perhaps gauge the depth of our faith by the determination with which we commit ourselves to prayer. Prayer is love in action, and love is faith in action.

Hope

"There remain Faith, Hope and Love, and the greatest of these is Love." If love is the greatest, we would probably agree that faith comes next, with the bronze medal going to hope. It is a great thing to get a medal, and hope is a vital virtue. Because we are weak and life is long, we need hope to keep us going. Hope directs our gaze to God and keeps it there. It gives us assurance that He loves us and will take us to Himself. Never think that hope is optimism. It has nothing to do with the temperamental desire to believe that things will get better. Hope accepts the worst and can further accept that there is worse upon worst. But it can endure it all because of the promises of God. We can almost say that hope is a variant of faith, just as faith is a variant of love.

But the special quality of hope is to focus our gaze on what comes after death and how God will lead us with love and compassion up to that crucial moment in our lives. We have no idea what heaven is like. Jesus Himself has told us it has not entered into the human heart to imagine what God has prepared for those who love Him. In fact, all imagining turns out to be rather childish. Its reality we accept in faith, unimagined, cleave to with love and await in hope.

"Even though I walk through the valley of the shadow of death, I will fear no evil." That is hope, a personal conviction that God will see we come to no harm. More than that, this harm is only harm in a worldly sense. In the light of heaven, whatever seems harmful is only for our soul's health. Hope accepts all disaster, understands it as disaster, but knows that fundamentally it is irrelevant. It is so convinced of the goodness of God, of His compassionate love, that it will always remain steadfast. When we pray, we hope with complete confidence that God is giving Himself to us, loving and delighting in us, and we cannot even envisage disappointment. There is no proof, remember. Body and soul may feel we are wasting our time. Hope smiles and ignores them.

Peace

Peace, like joy, can be very easily misinterpreted as a state of mind. When we have no anxieties and our bodies are functioning satisfactorily, the resultant lack of tension presents itself to us as peace. This, of course, is a kind of peace, low grade, material and without substance. Change our circumstances, external or internal, and where is the peace?

The peace that matters for prayer is independent. It persists unaffected by financial difficulties, relationship problems or threats of serious disease. It does not block out the pain of these conditions. It rises above them. Your prayer may be tormented by the thoughts of your mortgage, of your child's problems at school, of your stomachache and headache and backache. All too often people say, "I was too sick to pray" or "I was too worried to pray." Rather we should say, "My prayer today is of a sick and worried person." It is you God wants to take to Himself in prayer, and if that is a you with shingles or a you with marriage problems, He is compassionate toward his child, but does not demand that the reality of life be discarded. You cannot step out of your real life with all its tensions into "a peace." God does not want you to. It would be a state of unreality. You bring these tensions to your prayer and turn away from them to God. That may mean a turning away at every second. It will not be a restful prayer, but it is a peaceful prayer, because that is your choice. What may feel like wounds are really only surface bruises, in that the essential you — what makes you tick — wants only Him, and will never be damaged. (How do I know that this is true? I do not know. I have no certainty if I rely on my own feelings or beliefs. This is what it means to trust God, who alone does know and will make it clear if we are in a state of self-deception.) Emotional flurries will always pass, but the peace of God endures.

Peace II

When we pray, we do not step out of the real world. It is only true prayer if we are completely within our own context, in all its grubbiness and incoherence and uncertainty. All of us live in what can be described as a moral jungle. What Grant Wood shows us in *Spring Turning* is the world as we would like it to be, the world as we somehow feel in God it should be (figure 13). The gentle hills billow beneath a blue sky, and everything is orderly. Soil and crops, trees and fences, the house, the windmill, the sheep, the plow—all exist in untroubled order. Merely to contemplate this scene gives an immense sense of satisfaction: "Ah, if only!"

Yet the moral meaning of this beautifully serene and ordered world is precisely what prayer will achieve within us. All our outward circumstances will remain as haphazard as before. But we ourselves will be drawn deeper and deeper into that peaceful security that Wood envisages. There are shadows in this perfect world, dark ones too, and the sky is not cloudless. But no one could look at this picture and feel the slightest frisson of dread or foreboding. The small farmer and his lovely land are infinitely protected, held in a rhythm that seems eternal. We may not feel—one cannot say this too often—any of this widespread serenity, but we can live in the conviction of it. God is peace.

Penance

When you read the lives of the saints (I am thinking now of Bishop Butler and his tradition of hagiography), it is extraordinary that the selling point, as it were, is the saints' devotion to penance. They lived on top of pillars (for example, Simon Stylites); they scourged themselves to fainting point or imposed the extremity of physical pain on their bodies (for example, Saint Cuthbert standing all night in freezing water); they fled in fear from physical beauty (for example, Saint Rose of Lima praying to God to destroy her physical loveliness and Saint Lucy asking to have her great luminous eyes wrenched out of their sockets).

One sometimes gets the impression that these saints were canonized because of their physical penances. Forget about love and prayer: one can deduce these, the reasoning goes, from the extremes to which they brought their bodies. Fast until you faint? You must love God. Go without sleep? Ah, what devotion! Today we are more dubious about these penitential extravaganzas. We still love them; we are deeply impressed by them. They still seem to bear their own credentials blazing bright on their foreheads, yet we have perhaps come to realize the element here of the extraordinary, the UFO, that essentially impresses us, not because it comes from God, but because it is bizarre, a seemingly spiritual version of the poltergeist. True faith is something very much deeper.

Even today many people seem to think that true religion is defined by giving up things. In a sense it is far easier to deny one's body than quietly and soberly to surrender your whole self for God's possessing. In Lent, how much easier it is to give up wine or chocolate than seriously to tackle our impatience. A friend of mine who was prepared to fast most rigorously in Lent was horrified when I suggested daily mass and half an hour's prayer instead. That she shrank from, compared to the athletic glory of a penitential fast. It is always not what we do, but why we do it. And our motive must always come from fixing our eyes solely on Jesus.

The self-denying penitent has the comfort of saying, "I inflict so much suffering upon myself—fasting, vigils, abstinences—surely I love Him?" Our Lord asks us to love without this reassurance. We set aside time for prayer, and more and more we try to orient our whole day to prayer, but we sacrifice the comfort—the paradoxical comfort—of physical discomfiture. Are we becoming holy? Leave it, this is God's business. Our business, again, is to accept the terrible simplicity of prayer, that accurate barometer of whether we want Him or not. Dear Lord, do for us what we cannot do for ourselves.

Holiness

If I were to define a saint, I would say that it is somebody completely illuminated by the love of God. Or I could say that it is somebody whom God totally possesses in prayer. There is no holiness without prayer. For that matter, there is no Christianity without prayer. If we believe in the God whom Jesus reveals to us as Father, then we stretch out to Him, and that yearning—always, remember, a yearning of the will not of the emotions—is prayer.

When Jesus urged us to become perfect as our heavenly Father is perfect, He was not speaking of something definable. To be perfect is to be complete. God is perfect in that He is completely the Godhead. There is one God and He is completely Himself. But there is not one humanity. We are all human in different ways. And, for us, perfection — to me rather an off-putting noun — can mean only becoming completely what we are meant to be. Each of us is called to an individual fulfillment that only God understands. Because we are all different, "perfection," which I would prefer to call "holiness," will be different for each of us. It will take into account our genetic weaknesses. It will allow for the areas in which we will never be objectively admirable, though we may have subjectively striven to the full extent that God desires.

Take Saint Peter — impetuous, given to rushes of blood to the head, wildly overestimating his own courage and faith, and yet within it all humbled and weeping — clinging to his Lord. Holiness for Peter did not mean becoming a different man: a wise, prudent, controlled man. It meant being the same old silly Peter, but one who progressively clung to Jesus and became His true disciple. Peter loved Jesus, not despite his weaknesses, but in them and through them.

Each of us is in some way a Peter, with weaknesses and strengths that we do not understand. It is Jesus who understands, who will show us in prayer what we must sacrifice and what He can purify into the strength of love. It is in prayer that we explore these mysterious dimensions. It is not we who explore, but God who draws us ever further into what He sees could be our completion, our perfection (*perfectum*, "having been made complete").

This is not our business; this is God's business. It is for us to surrender ourselves to Him. It is for God to make something of this and to use it for the health of the world. Regarding prayer as "our own" is prideful folly. It is Jesus who prays in us. It is Jesus who surrenders us to the Father. It is Jesus who takes us beyond all we can understand and makes us a conduit of His Spirit.

There have been times when there has been a belief in possession by the devil, the evil spirit. We who cling to Jesus believe in possession by God, the Holy Spirit. However poor and humble our prayer, this is its aim: that God will take possession of us, live within us, give His love to the world through us.

Dear friends who are reading this book, let us long for this, let us hope for this, let us believe that this will happen, not because we are good, but because God is.

About the Author

Sister Wendy Beckett, a member of a teaching order of nuns, the Order of Notre Dame, is well known for her insight into the history of art. Her BBC television series has been shown on PBS, and she is the author of several best-selling books. Along with her disciplined life as a nun, she devotes her contemplative life to the careful study of art.